# THE DAO OF DOUG 2:
# THE ART OF DRIVING A BUS

Keeping Zen in San Francisco Transit: A Line Trainer's Guide

DOUGLAS MERIWETHER

**BALBOA.**
PRESS
A DIVISION OF HAY HOUSE

Balboa Press books may be ordered through booksellers or by contacting:

Balboa Press
A Division of Hay House
1663 Liberty Drive
Bloomington, IN 47403
www.balboapress.com
1 (877) 407-4847

Because of the dynamic nature of the Internet, any web addresses or links contained in this book may have changed since publication and may no longer be valid. The views expressed in this work are solely those of the author and do not necessarily reflect the views of the publisher, and the publisher hereby disclaims any responsibility for them.

The author of this book does not dispense medical advice or prescribe the use of any technique as a form of treatment for physical, emotional, or medical problems without the advice of a physician, either directly or indirectly. The intent of the author is only to offer information of a general nature to help you in your quest for emotional and spiritual well-being. In the event you use any of the information in this book for yourself, which is your constitutional right, the author and the publisher assume no responsibility for your actions.

All images courtesy of the author.

Print information available on the last page.

ISBN: 978-1-4525-2280-7 (sc)
ISBN: 978-1-4525-2282-1 (hc)
ISBN: 978-1-4525-2281-4 (e)

Library of Congress Control Number: 2014917274

Balboa Press rev. date: 03/07/2017

The views contained herein do not necessarily reflect those of the SFMTA or its employees.

"Better three hours too early, than one minute too late"
– William Shakespeare

———

Special Thanks to baristas Angela, Chan, Brian, Data,
Jaime, Karla, Kim, Luis, Memo, Mike, et. al. for providing
the dark roast coffee as fuel for writing this book.

———

Whether you take mass transit or drive, either in San Francisco
or elsewhere, this book offers philosophical wisdom beyond
the overt advice on how to be a better passenger or driver, and
how to deal with traffic jams and difficult personalities. The
sequel to the Dao of Doug is about the art of remaining peaceful
and maintaining dignity when the going gets tough.

Jackie Cohen,
member of the Board of Directors,
National Lesbian and Gay Journalists Association

———

"I've been riding Muni for my whole life and, as an SF Weekly
reporter, delving deep into its inner workings for many years. It's
not always a pretty picture. Actually, it's rarely a pretty picture. So
that's why Driver Doug's tales are such a pleasure. They're the often
painfully honest testimonials of a man who really gives a damn.
A man who strives to achieve Zen while operating a Muni bus is
worth getting to know. San Franciscans get on the bus. And then
they get off. But Doug is there for the long haul, pulling in, pulling
out, and motoring, ever closer, to Zen. May he reach it soon.

Joe Eskenazi,
SF Weekly staff writer and columnist

# CONTENTS

# WHY I WROTE THIS BOOK

I was asked why I wrote a book about being a bus driver in San Francisco. The first reason was in answer to why I am here. "We are all here to do what we are all here to do," as the Oracle tells Neo in the *Matrix* trilogy. Being of service was and is my first motive to get what I learned down on paper. As a guide for those who follow me at the job, I hope to provide a higher vantage point from which to see what lies ahead on the road. And not just with the drive-cam evidence at a Skelley (disciplinary) hearing! To get us on the same page. And for the public at large to get an understanding, a wakeup call, how to smooth the ride.

Where we place the door seems to baffle most intending passengers. The distraction of showing a transfer at an awkward, unsafe moment also causes complaints to arise from our aggravated tone of voice, with a complete lack of understanding of why. Our passion about safety is a first priority, and the challenge is in trying to relay much experience in a short span of time. This relay is what this book is all about. We have reasons for why we do what we do, and if this is understood, another angel can be with us on the bus, and not in the complaint cue.

When patrons rush to the door, they are just as unsure about what to expect from the bus driver as I am of them. If anything written here stirs controversy (although not my intent), it would be worth it to get into a conversation about what has worked and what has not: To see through eyes of interconnectedness, not isolated in our car with the windows up (except for a hand sticking out with the single middle finger in the air as it passes by the bus) is my hope.

The "caution and reinstruct" love letter from our superintendent after an incident, comes without the necessary clarity about our part, *and their part,*

1

in causing the conflict. It is the proposed solution for next time and an opportunity, through our Zen-like mastery, to state safety needs without an angry or harsh tone.

Preconceived notions or attachment to something else is what's usually behind a service complaint. It is often not what is said, but the tone in which it was said. In the flash-of-the-pan moment, this becomes almost impossible; but on the pages of this tome, a "space cushion" remains.

This space cushion we are trained to keep around our bus at all times goes a long way toward explaining why we are splitting the lane or driving down both lanes of traffic in the Mission or on Van Ness. We are avoiding car doors, skaters, bike riders, and the person with the door open at their parked car. We can't answer your question right now because we are busy looking at the show in front of, and up to, one-to-two blocks ahead. Now sit down and be still, please. Or as you sometimes say to us, "Shut-up and drive the bus," and "Just do your job." Surprise, surprise. *We are* and you're not helping!

I am continually returned to the state of abashment at the attempts to destroy the self-possession or self-confidence of my integrity and job experience. Someone enters and alights before I have a chance to answer and complains of discourtesy. A motorist rushes ahead, only to block the lane to wait for a parking space. A "fixie" on his bike passes on the right and stands in the crosswalk, preventing a right turn on red. It's an assigned penalty in a love letter that proposes no solution. The other reason for this book is to respond to the continual bombardment from the press, the public, and those in "authority," of our operators' response, "Try a week, *a day* behind the wheel, and *then* tell me what you think!"

In the past year, I have received feedback from passengers, coworkers, and other, newer operators, and I hope this follow-up sequel answers the questions I still get about issues or topics not found in book one, *Finding Zen*. The glossary in the back of this sequel is a tool to help understand words with which you may be unfamiliar. A *Skelley*, just used above, for example, is that first part of progressive discipline between the manager, the union representative, and the self that tries to follow due process leading to the penalty box.

Fortunately, classes are given on a regular basis in the training department to keep the information fresh. We have AR training (Accident Review), VTT class (Verified Transit Training), and requalification for those who haven't been behind the wheel for sixty days. This *Line Trainer's Guide* is just another point of information to get us on the same page. When I see the small coincidence of right action and joy around me on the bus and on the street, I get such a smile and a laugh and realize I am in the right place at the right time.

This book, and the stories within its chapters, are from intense passions released in the never-dull moments of driving a ten-ton vehicle on overhead wires in San Francisco. The life of a trolley operator contains all the challenge I ever need in a job. Thank you for reading. Thank you for riding!

# THE COLAS AND SALT POSSE

In receiving feedback from new operators who were interested in my first book about finding Zen, they thought that the "guidebook" would contain factual information about passing the tests for getting a class B license. This chapter is a response. One of the more stressful tests in becoming a qualified operator in the state is to pass the air brake test. The air brake test can be stressful, especially if memorization skills are rusty. The acronyms, *COLA*, and *SALT POSSE*, helped me get the air brake check lined up in the correct order so the qualified state inspector would be put at ease and would, therefore, put me at ease to increase the chances of passing the test.

Knowing that COLA is the first part of the air brake test, **C** stands for cut-in, **O** for cut-out, **L** for LAWD, the low air warning device, and **A** for air or the beginning of the air leakage rate tests.

**C**—After chocking the rear wheel on the right, turn on master control, and between pumps in the service brake, you are lowering the air on the needle to get the compressor to cut-in and begin restoring air to the tanks. The cut-in should occur at or slightly below 85 psi (pounds per square inch), and the cut-out should be at 125 psi. *During the test, you must state that you are seeing the needle start to rise to confirm that the air governor has cut in.*

**O**—Stop pumping the brake to bleed the air, and then wait for cut-out. To confirm this and to pass the test, you must say, *The needle has stopped rising.* This occurs at 125 psi.

**L**—Now comes the low air warning device. Continue to pump and bleed so that the needles drop out of operating range and down to 55-to-75 psi. This is when an alarm should sound. Continue until the parking brake pops up at around 40 psi.

**A**—This is an automatic safety feature that will hold the coach when air is dropping. Let the air rebuild, and get ready to perform the air leakage rate tests, **S.A.L.T.** Always state air in pounds per square inch and not just say the number 85 or 125, but 85 psi or 125 psi.

SALT is an acronym for the standard air leakage test. This begins by turning off master control and placing your foot on the service brake for one minute and watching the air gauge needle to see that it does not drop more than 3 psi. [The minimum brake test, for example, where we put our foot down on the power pedal to see if the bus won't move with the parking brake on, has been cut. The equipment from the Czech Republic, the ETI Skoda, fails this test, as the hill climber was built into the points of power on this bus. The hill climber helps us up steep hills.]

We then go on to **POSSE:** I am going to check my air leakage for the **P**, parking brake, the **O**, open lines, the **S**, static air leakage test, the **S**, service brake, and the **E**, emergency brake. The last two, **S** and **E**, are called the rolling brake tests where you accelerate and use the service brake in a smooth, controlled stop and in an abrupt stop. The emergency brake test is applied to see if the coach is held by the brakes; it used to be a part of the minimum brake test whereby you would put on the parking brake and then depress the power pedal to see if the bus would roll or not. But if you do state the items of POSSE to the instructor, you let him know that you've been around a while and have knowledge of the requirements of previous years.

I would always be confused about the word *static*. What the heck does that mean? When coupled with its opposite, *dynamic*, I realized static means not changing or not moving, like the dynamic brakes that engage after the air brakes when coming to a complete stop. The air brakes are then what hold the coach on the hill by use of the hill holder. This toggle button holds the coach by the air brakes so that you can rest your foot on the brake pedal. This switch is part of the interlock system used by the back doors and is active when the green light is on above the rear door. The door dial and hill holder both hold the coach by the air brakes, but the service brake should be used before a smooth start or stop. The rear of the coach is where the front spring is compressed or uncompressed and is the primary system for keeping the coach stopped. The secondary system is in the front. The two gauges you see on the dash have two needles. The white is always the rear. It is the primary brake system. The spring brake is another name for this white needle, primary air brake system. In older flyer coaches, the green needle is for the rear air.

The secondary system is signified by the red needle and is for the front tanks. This one is usually moving behind the other needle, depending on where the air compressor is and how far the lines and tanks are from the compressor. That loud pop you guys hear is when the tanks are full, and cut-out has been reached. This pop, however, is no longer a part of the DMV test, as other secondary systems on certain manufacturers of equipment have surge suppression for kneelers, stabilizer levelers, or water vapor "dryers" that can make a similar pop sound and not reflect that the primary tank is full. Once again, the new statement you must make to the DMV State Instructor to pass the air governor cut-out test is to say, *The needle has stopped rising.* The pop you may or may not hear can give you the clue, but you must base your observation on the needle and not the pop.

As a motorist, I never knew that the service brake was the correct name for what most people just called the brake. The emergency brake is also called the parking brake. So I came to believe that if I was ever to talk to a professional driver (perhaps at a truck stop), the terms service brake and parking brake would telegraph status above Class C. So much is understood with knowing how brakes work and what items are needed to check with preoperation that, seeing a motorist pull away on a cold day without defrosting or scraping the windows, shows a neglect that is not safe or professional. This brings us to the first part of taking the bus out as a professional, the pre-op or preoperational checklist before going into revenue service.

# PRE-OP

Muni instructors are good at this, as are all state-qualified trainers. This test is much easier when you are in the bus and moving slowly around the points to be covered. As long as you pan around with a mental note of where you are, you simply describe everything as you walk around. The required things you must now say to yourself are as follows:

**Mirrors:** I will adjust them later. **Tires:** I cannot have retread, regrooved, or recapped ones on the front, but I can on the back, and they must be the same size, same type. I would check between the rear tandem tires to see if there is debris. If I had a mallet, I would check air pressure. Do not kick the tires. This does not gain extra credit.

For the front of the coach, a *W* pattern from ID lights to the wipers and across works best. Looking down the side of the coach, verbalize that you are checking the windows to make sure they are secure.

Upon entering the coach and after checking aisles, windows, ER exit latches, roof hatches, chime cords, hand holds, seats and stanchions, wheel chair area, fire extinguisher, wheel blocks, safety cone, *close the door and put on your seatbelt.*

Important things to remember on a daily basis are to check the rope tension on the poles in the back of the trolley. The poles have a specific slot at forty five degrees from the angle on the roof whereby the pole can be lowered to inspect the collectors, the carbon in the brasserie, and the shunt wires and swivel rotation of the collector. The collectors are the two swivels at the end of the pole that collect the power. The shunt wires are the two wires that move this power down the pole to the inverter so the bus system can be powered.

It quickly becomes obvious that other fixed objects can block you from lowering the pole to eye level, so whenever checking this (even on a track in the yard), you may have to move to a more favorable location. It's important to have both wires down when doing this, unless you want to see how far you can fly off the ground when your body becomes the ground for the 600 volts of direct current. Not a good idea to be doing this in a puddle of water in the rain with metal toe guards in your shoes.

Setting up the coach in the seat requires more than what you are taught for pre-op by the state test. You do need to see if master control is in the correct setting if the bus has been turned on by the yard starter and that the fare box is not blocked. Setting the pattern, the destination, and the run sign all take time each morning or at relief. These procedures are not part of regular training to pass the test. If the DVAS (Digital Voice Activated System) is making a recurring announcement, the run sign may not update. Also, if the buttons on the DVAS are sticky or picky, it may take extra time to get displays correct. The wheel blocks and cones are a big deal. If you have no cone or wheel block, that is a warning sign that the bus may be trouble. If the bus needed these during the last shift, why are they missing now? Did the shop take them? Were they used somewhere else? The odds you will need them go way up if the bus is missing them.

Inevitably, what is not checked is missing or is what you will need later on in the day. Keep your Zen! Keep your job!

# MIRROR, MIRROR

This is a great follow-up chapter, especially after an accident. In fact, it was after an accident that I had to relearn the art of mirror placement and view. The subtleties in rocker arm angle and tightness of the joints make for a challenge to get the best view from the seatback. Changing the elevation of the seat and the distance from the pedals can cut off a small, but critical, sliver of blind spot view towards the rear that becomes really important really fast when leaving the curb or passing double-parked vehicles.

In training, the famous wheel block example comes to mind. The instructor places a wheel block even with the footprint of the rear tire and asks the student to center the wheel block in the bottom view of the flat mirror from the driver's seat. The view in the rectangle of our mirror should place the wheel block at the center of the rear tire in the middle of the bottom frame of the mirror. Seat adjustment also comes into play. Am I high and tight or low-rider and reclined?

This makes a difference in revenue service at the relief point. Is the operator I relieve shorter or taller? I can either adjust the seat to keep the mirrors aligned, or I can raise or lower the seat and then tilt the mirrors. The rush to keep the beat may have to wait for this critical pause when "sliding seats."

I usually keep the seat in the same position as the operator I relieve to see how it fits my body first. But I check the elevation of the curbside mirrors immediately and use the joystick to change the angle on a mirror, if it no longer fits my height in the chair. I don't get cramps or twists in my back or legs from riding in the same position day after day, week after week when I change how I sit and how I angle the mirrors. With the older buses, it's usually easier to adjust the seat rather than the mirrors.

Most of us have found the universal position for the mirrors on the older buses and have come to believe that an attempt to move the rocker arm and angle of the mirror becomes like the cartoon of sawing off legs on a chair to keep it from rocking. One tap on the mirror can cause more problems than it's worth. Moving the chair to fit the mirror is usually okay if my legs can reach the power pedal and brake without any play. I know that taking the time to get the mirrors right is my highest priority.

Right now, I am seeing that my interior mirror angle needs lowering so that I can get better coverage of the seats in front of the middle or rear door. I have been switched on to a "drive cam mode" in my mind's eye. That is to say, I am missing passenger complaints because I am scanning what is going on within the coach. Mirrors are not only helpful for scanning traffic hazards outside of the bus, but also for what is going on inside. The miracle of the appearance of having eyes behind my head or intuitively opening the door without a ring comes from how I set my mirrors. Keeping Zen is much easier than guessing about what may happen next.

# LPO

The installation of cameras on the front windscreen has had one beneficial effect. Those monitoring our pull-out time see how much extra time is required to move deficient coaches out of the way. With trolleys at Potrero, we have so many coaches dead on the tracks that we are trapped in a canyon or gauntlet of unmoving buses, such that if the lead coach in front of us is caught in restrictive mode at start-up, we are blocked from pulling out on time.

A good yard starter is found turning on coaches well in advance of their pull-out in the morning to see if a reboot is necessary. The installation of computers and memory chips on buses may be great for global positioning monitoring and data checking brake function, speed, and door-opens, but these devices can create hassles with morning sickness on the equipment when it has been a cold night with heavy fog. Moisture adhering to carbon on the various components and electrical sensor points creates annoying warnings, such as hot body, that cut into the calm of morning pull-out. (I have always wanted a hot body, but not on my assigned coach!)

In the afternoon, finding a good coach can be like hide-and-seek, and I was blessed with being able to talk to my leader on her cut-in pull-out as to why she was having difficulty making the pull-out on time. The secret to making sure all is well is to allow for more than ten minutes of extra time when arriving to the pre-op point. If this is not possible, then communicate the problem in a way that does not ruffle feathers. Not a good idea to upset the shop and crew working on your equipment before you pull out in the morning.

Oh gee, the coach is in restrictive mode, or the inductive dial is turned to the right. Oh, the coach was turned on in day run. Did I check to see if I was on night run with all my lights on? And the pre-op list goes on. The key to having no trouble has been to show up early to make sure the coach is on and not in restricted mode. I have to check the master dial and make sure the coach is not in neutral on the ETI or in neutral on the Flyer. I also have to make sure the bus was not left on in epu (emergency power unit or battery mode) last night, or else I am not going anywhere. The precious extra fifteen minutes we are given on our paycheck to pre-op the coach comes in handy when we have to get the yard starter to call the shop to assist us with a jump or a reboot of the circuit board to get us going. If I wait until the last moment to reprogram the fare box, I could hear a nasty alarm that the box is open or has no power.

As creatures of habit, we usually save the fare box to last, but this, too, can lead to a late pull-out. So the key is to show up before pull-out to make sure the bus is in gear, in power, and programmed from head sign to fare box so that no surprises await. Checking the wipers to see that they actually clean the window and the mirrors and that they are in a good alignment, can also dog us in being late. Especially if it has been dry, and the wipers haven't been used for a long time. The wash rack throws mirror arms out of alignment.

If the wipers were left on at a terminal during a misty rain, the window can be smeared with dull blades. And finally, deployment of the lift is icing on the cake to determine if I will have a day of service or a day of waiting for the shop and giving the bus and operator behind me a double passenger load.

I am happy to say I have kept the Zen in pulling out on time over the years and have had very few LPOs to my name. Cutting in on the line is an art in and of itself. Just as with a switchback, entering the line a few minutes late or behind time is a good idea for not getting ahead of oneself, which is to say that an empty bus moves up in headway faster than the following coach that already has a load. Being aware of this helps keep the Zen with your follower.

# TIMED TRANSFERS

If you are taking a bus in the wee hours of the morning, a good place to find out where to go to meet one is at a bus shelter with a map of the transit system. In the corner of the map is a gray box that shows the owl lines. Owl lines are the bus routes that operate 24/7 and in the period between 2:00 a.m. and 6:00 a.m. The schedule of the owl buses does not change from weekdays to weekends, and generally, you can count on their arrival every thirty minutes. Because no traffic or construction delays exist in the early morning, the schedule for these buses is very accurate. I have found in taking the N Judah at 4:30 a.m. to be so accurate that I could set my watch to its schedule when it arrived at Haight and Clayton.

Because the late night buses run so smoothly, certain crossroads or transfer points exist between these two lines and are designated timed transfers. Not too many people notice this detail on the map. And perhaps, very few ever need to know when the N Judah comes inbound in relation to the 22 Fillmore. But when you really need to know, and it's zero dark thirty, and you see the 22 turning the corner on to 16th from Church as your N Judah pulls up two blocks behind the 22 at Market, the bummer is a hard one to get over. The 22 and N are not a timed transfer and miss each other by about three minutes. Ouch. Add another half hour to your morning commute to your 5:00 a.m. start time at the job.

I just looked at a new map and headway timetable in a new shelter and now see that the timed transfer symbol has been removed from the owl map! There goes another chapter idea down the drain before it even went to print! Though Muni (short for Municipal Railway) does not now recognize timed transfers between buses at night, that does not necessarily mean buses do not meet at certain corners. The 90 Owl and L Taraval still may meet at Market and Van Ness. As a bus driver aware of these timed transfers in the past, I am more likely to wait for the crossing bus, having knowledge about passengers wishing to make the connection.

Unfortunately, with the reduction in service and with new hires, this connection is lost. And the reality of losing a half hour in an early morning commute to open up a coffee shop or warehouse is lost upon newer drivers. The fact that the new map no longer shows timed transfers is a wee hour loss that few, if any, realize, but it's of great importance to those few who need to get around in the early hours.

My first free copy of the *Zen Zone* went to my coffee shop manager, who had to transfer in the Richmond to get inbound to Geary and Fillmore to open up at zero dark thirty. I told him he could use the hardcover addition as a means for getting the attention of the operator stalling at Park Presidio. He finally gave up trying to open the store on time and now works near his house. The travails of those traveling to work early are increased by service cuts. The precision and timing of transfers is lost when gaps occur between transfers, and ridership suffers. The cuts that occurred in 2010 "cost" riding time at night. It was the same with the cutbacks to the terminals on the 24. Every time a terminal is shortened, ridership declines. Ask anyone on the 2 Clement, with its shorter terminal at Park Presidio and 15th Avenue. Cutting terminals is the first step in eliminating a line altogether.

So, the essence is if you have to travel on a regular basis, get to know the regular operator, and get the times of a critical jumping off point. If you miss the next bus, find out from that operator when his or her leader goes by. It is possible that, over time, you can make the connection, as the other operator will wait for you. When lines are not adjusted, the chances increase that the same operator will stay with that run after a new signup. This helps with consistency and predictability. Even if Muni does not now acknowledge timed transfers, it does not mean you cannot still make them between lines.

A good rule of thumb is not to wait crosstown in the avenues, but head inbound first. Then take the 22 headed inbound away from the barn. The main thing is to try different routes to see which one works for the shortest commute.

Today, agencies work together to keep their All-Nighter runs to meet at Van Ness and Market. This would be a huge score for keeping Zen in mass transit. If you raise the fare, add more time onto the transfer.

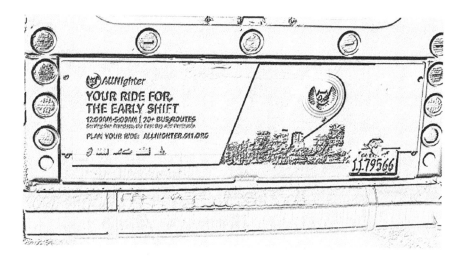

# TRANSFER CUT

As a rule of thumb, each trip we make on a line is about forty five minutes long, with a ten-minute recovery. On longer lines such as the 14, trip length is fifty five minutes with a five-minute chance to go to the bathroom. So each lap down and back takes an hour. Our transfers are to be cut so that one has ninety minutes from time of purchase to use the transfer to take another bus on another line that crosses the one on which you start. Since our trips only last for half of this time, there should be ample time to take another bus, even if you board at terminal A and go all the way to terminal B. A ninety minute transfer time is double the time it takes us to make one trip from Daly City to the Ferry Plaza or from Dogpatch to Marina Green. No brainer, right? Ha!

Many riders believe they should be able to board, get off, run errands, go to a meeting, see a friend, and then have the time to go back for a round-trip.

If their meeting lasts an hour or more, then one transfer won't hack it in making it back to the original boarding point, especially if the transit time is close to a full trip. I usually ask them to consider buying a fast pass. No change, no looking for coins, no problems in running out of time. The response is, "I don't ride enough to make it worthwhile."

As an equalizer for value, I believe we should extend the transfer time to our riders so they can make a round-trip on one transfer, instead of having to pay twice. This should help to minimize delays at the fare box. Our hidden rule of thumb is to change the cut in transfer time at our terminal and to put this time cut two hours from our leaving time at our next terminal. This gives those boarding at the beginning of our line plenty of time to run an errand at considerable distance from where they boarded and to use the same transfer on the way back. Increasing the time given on the transfer would be a politically correct way to add value when the next fare increase passes.

From the point of those who pay, it looks like the extra quarter should be added to the discount fare of seventy-five cents. These are the riders who are not under time constraints, such as those who pay full fare to make it to work. The gratitude expressed for our transit system comes more often than not from those paying full fare. Several levels of discount fare payers have an attitude about paying at the box. One way of simplifying this conflict of class struggle would be to eliminate the cash fare altogether, and have a magnetic strip or a scan-only as a method of payment. This would greatly speed up boarding and transit times.

But people are creative in ways to get past the fare box and not pay at all. If I am very busy, I let some of these transgressions pass, but it doesn't mean I am not aware you are scamming the system. It begins by saving your transfer from yesterday. If you boarded the coach later in the day, you have a longer transfer, and if you place your thumb over the date, it looks like a good transfer. This doesn't work on the first of the month when the transfer changes color. Still, there are a few diehards who try it anyway.

The other way to block the ID of the transfer is if you purchase a transfer earlier in the day. The transfer is held like a cup so that your hand blocks the bottom strip indicating the time of expiry. Finally, there are those who have been burned in the past by fare inspectors, who hold the transfer in such a disguise mode and then lash out at the driver when asked to pay the fare. They move their hand to show that the transfer is valid and attempt to discourage the operator from questioning the fare. This is how riders train operators not to check the transfer.

I remember when I was new to the city and put in coins every trip. I did not want to commit to a whole month's pass. But as soon as I did, I found I used the bus more often than not, and that the simplicity of a pass was worth the freedom of not having to search for money every time I boarded. The rub is having enough money to buy the pass when rent is due. As an operator, humility goes a long way toward remembering the challenge of paying for transportation in such an expensive city. I would also do well to remember that our city fathers have serious challenges in making ends meet to pay for the maintenance on all of our fleet. Keeping the Zen can be the hardest part of staying calm in the seat behind the wheel.

# NOT A BUS... A PERSON DRIVING A BUS

One of the most frustrating aspects of the bustle and tussle of a large, dense city is just missing a connection. This chapter is for the regular transit rider who may still be missing transfers to another bus. This situation can be averted by following one simple rule. Your desire to catch that trolley bus actually hinges, not on the caricature of one massive entity called a Municipal Transit Agency, but rather on an individual seated behind the wheel of a car. Yes, we call coaches or cars by their number, and it is okay to call a bus a car, such as car number 5505. If you are aware of car numbers, chances are you have a good handle on understanding the system. If your awareness extends to run number, car number, cap number, and line number, then your status is elevated to that of a Muni god. By reading this book, you, too, can be elevated unto that heavenly status. Gods can get angry. Gods can cause major damage. Gods can cause a rush of change. But when they are benevolent as angels, good things can happen.

Most of us have been given the incorrect model on how to affect change. Heck, I can't even spell the distinction correctly! Do you desire an effect or an affect? We believe that expending a burst of loud, hostile energy is a fast way to make change happen. Or, anger can be harbored for years, yet nothing changes. We become comfortable with our anger, nursing and polishing it into a fine object that can become attractive to all who encounter it. I know I have loved my deepest and longest-held resentments against a large organization and loved telling others about these over happy hour. Now, however, I write them down on my inventory list with my twelve-step recovery sponsor.

My most exciting challenge is to transform this wonderfully polished and shiny resentment about missed transfers into a missive about the approaches to catching a bus and the mistakes people make in doing so.

If you are on a one-shot deal, then all I can give you are the facial expressions or body language that will cause me to wait for you and hope that they work on a transfer you may never have to make again.

## The Wounded Kitty

Aw, poor baby. Are you all alone on the cold, wet corner without a warm, dry bus for shelter? This works if I have room and time, and I know there is no bus behind me. A smile at the last minute works great if timed correctly. A Homer Simpson "d'oh" or one loud, profane exclamation also works if timed just as the front door passes by. This technique works great when traffic is light or nonexistent. Twilights and Sundays are good prospect times for wounded kitty. If you're not young and pretty, a sigh of sadness with quivering cane uplifted to an invisible Kaiser also works. Dropping the shoulders Charlie Brown-style after Lucy also works wonderfully. But note that these all require the eye contact of acknowledging that it is a person driving a bus, and not just a bus.

## The Plea Bargain

This was used in the movie *Speed*. Annie makes it to the doomed bus as Sam, the bus driver, jokes that this boarding point is not at the bus stop. I have expanded this with the train and plane analogy of questions: "Where do you catch a train?" "At a train station." "Where do you get on a plane?" "At an airport." "And where do we get a bus?" Some of you latecomers are so puffed up with pride that you may never get on a bus. But if you pronate yourself, as if praying to the Muni god of nigh, the transit operator, grace has been known to open the back door (occasionally). This would be a good chapter for a movie. I wish I could call up some clips on the plea bargain. The plea bargain can come silently with the eyes, or with a huge, loud, profane word. The more over-the-top, the better!

## The Dignitary

This only works with blessed folk, those who attend church regularly and have a comfortable sense of self-righteousness that does not infringe on others. Those who pray regularly without self-centered fear can stop a bus from any location just by a simple turn of the head and a smile. It is always a wonderful rush to pick up someone like this—rare indeed, but all the more meaningful. Quality, not quantity is definitely the Dao of this pick-up.

## The Lost Puppy

Unfortunately, these are the most dramatic and visceral because of their stand-alone nature. If you are traveling from the East Bay for a job interview, for example, and are new to the system, the time you are allowing for transfers may be inadequate. The image of successfully dashing across the street to a streetcar from a trolley is easy to get, especially if you have heard our service is frequent. The reality of the situation is that you need to add twenty minutes for every mode or bus transfer to your first-time journey. As you become familiar with the transfers, transit time can be reduced, such that a trip that may have taken two hours and twenty minutes to complete can be shaved down to forty five minutes.

We operators become aware of the places where intending passengers ask us for a destination behind us. On crosstown routes, we see that by a BART station people board buses going in the opposite direction from where they need to reach their destination. By traveling for fifteen or twenty minutes in the wrong direction, they can add an hour to their travel time. This is sometimes a sad and frustrating conversation. It can throw off my concentration of staying alert to road hazards. This unfocused energy can be just as harmful to the bus driver as it is to your missed appointment or interview.

If you have been given an address, it is important to search for it on a map system so you have a good idea as to the corner where you need to wait. If a delay creates a gap in trolleys, this lack of knowing where to stand can immediately add twenty minutes. Waiting for the wrong bus and then changing direction, can create a bombshell at the door of the next bus. Keep the Zen by knowing at which corner to wait.

There can be four different lines on each different corner, with the same bus line going in two different directions on either side. Such is the case at Jackson and Fillmore, where people chronically wait on Fillmore instead of Jackson to take an outbound 24 to the Castro or Bayview. Seeing the sign post is not enough. You need to know which direction the bus is going. Asking others at the stop is a good idea, especially if the buses are running late on a weekend afternoon.

# CLOAK OF INVISIBILITY

If you would like to see a magic trick or illusion played out day after day, look no further than a ride on 14 Mission. The secret of becoming invisible is to sit in a wheelchair, particularly in a large group. The more, the merrier. It matters not where you sit on the sidewalk in the wheelchair. Those intending to board are only interested in their own desire. The thought of waiting for others or considering a need other than their own, does not compute. We have our "blinders" on and don't notice the changing conditions around us, such as someone with special needs waiting or approaching the bus stop after we have arrived.

In order to be of service, I need to walk that fine line of allowing those waiting to board first to "awaken" to see the person in the wheelchair who may be behind them or to the side. I have to be on guard with my tone of voice and how I express myself. *It is important to note that, from the driver's perspective, most conflict arises when approaching the front door from behind and to the right.* The blind spot is larger when the doors are open, because they partially block the side and rear views. Hiding behind the open doors causes hurt feelings.

I have an incredible opportunity to be a guide. Sometimes, it is simpler to let those passengers board first if the time between buses is short. If the number of those intending increases beyond four or five, with more boarding in the rear, loading the chair first is best. Those who are allowed up the front steps first usually sit down in the first two chairs under the wheel well and block the aisle. Others sit down in the flip-up seats where the wheelchair needs to secure. Young people with ear buds on and others with children enter through the middle door and sit in the wheelchair area, inattentive to my request to make room.

23

This is when I find it simpler to get up and face them with hand signals to rise. Raising the flip-up seats myself, before the chair lift is used, is the fastest way to get going if the person in the chair is alone and has no help, or if no passenger on board helps to raise the seats. Most of the time as operators, we don't have to get out to raise the seats because someone else offers help. Other times, help is available, but few know how to pull down and away to unlock the seats to raise them for the wheelchair. This is when I need to convey patience and cheerfulness and demonstrate how to lift the seats. I choose to believe that I am "lighting a candle" for others to see.

I am powerless over controlling passengers on my bus, but I also have a responsibility to those who need to get where they are going in a timely fashion. The biggest challenge I face today is to balance these needs without going over the top in anger and frustration and to keep the coach moving without a fall on board or a security incident. Humor can go a long way in diffusing a tense situation, but there are those who are so broken in spirit or illness who do not want help and are unable to think of anyone other than their own selves. Humor here does not work. It is perceived as an affront.

Most riders in wheelchairs have the faculty and support they need to obtain the equipment they require to be mobile. Others are unable to walk without support or must arrange for a special-needs transit, yet they insist that Muni take them back and forth, unaware of the impact they are having on the line. Still others insist I call the police over any small, perceived trespass, without regard for the welfare of those needing to get to their destination.

Case in point. A man at 16th and Mission attempts to block my coach and tells me to call the police. Another man, who was arguing with this man, just put his bike on the rack and entered through the rear door with a baby stroller loaded with his personal belongings. "He has my stroller!" says the first man. I beckon the man in the street to my window and suggest he ride with me in the back. The second man yells profanity at the man on the street and throws the stroller out the back door.

"He'll get what he's got coming to him," the first man responds calmly, walking to the sidewalk to retrieve his stroller. I nod in agreement. Sure enough, this angry man forgets to take his bike off the rack at 6th Street, where he rushes to get his belongings off without the stroller. He walks away with a nice woman in a wheelchair, who had plenty of time to board when the two were arguing at 16th Street. I ask the two bouncers on the corner club to remind the angry man that I'll be back in half an hour in the other direction so he can claim his bike. They nod in agreement.

When I get back to 6th Street, here is a different man, smiling and at peace as he removes his bike from the rack. God does not work in mysterious ways. Especially when I try to do the right thing! Another police call saved for another day. Another incident report after work unwritten. I can make my timed transfer just before 3:00 a.m. and catch my ride home.

Unfortunately, those with aimless purpose sometimes seem to have such a large sense of entitlement. I am at a loss on how to tame this beast. I have to say as little as possible and light the candle for another time, another place. *Don't feed the pigeons* is code for *keep quiet*. It goes against my Gemini nature to defer and delay a conversation about choosing where to sit, and this is a key reason for writing this book. I hope this message gets out to those who are regular riders, so that problems go away.

A recent spate of fights over seating in the front area of the bus has me thinking about how to clear this crunch zone before conflict develops. As agent Smith tells Neo in the movie, *Matrix*, "Do you hear that, Neo? It is the sound of inevitability." Not unlike a train approaching in the subway tunnel, lack of available space increases a head-on collision. This crunch zone always occurs in the Inner Mission and by Van Ness and Market. Thank you, Director of Transit, for locking seats in the upright position!

The other cloak of invisibility problem I find over seating and right of way is the passenger with ear buds on, occupying two seats with a coat or bag over another seat. The ear buds act as an invisibility shield: *You can't talk to me because I can't hear you. Especially if my eyes are closed!*

I sat next to this girl who adds to drama because she takes an aisle seat, covers the window seat, and becomes unavailable for talk as the bus fills up to capacity. If someone sits down on her coat, a battle of wills can ensue. *It is always a good idea to ask before entering someone's zone of personal space, as is being alert when seats are no longer available. This is a problem if you can't hear us because your ear buds are on, and you appear to be asleep.* Overcoming the fear of losing aisle space and seats for seniors has been a long and challenging journey for this transit operator in San Francisco. When you board, especially with a bike, or when others are nearby, unhook an ear bud by the fare box and keep the Zen going. Thanks!

# THE KNEELER

"You're supposed to lower the kneeler for seniors," or "Thanks for lowering the steps," sarcastically spoken *after* departing to the sidewalk does not help much. A request for the kneeler with a condescending tone (as if I'm a mind reader) after ascending or descending, may not reflect where my attention is focused at the time. The rule is to request the kneeler *before* alighting or stepping up. We are not in the know about the status of your hip joint, your back, your neck, your legs, and so on, if we have not seen you before.

We try to gauge need based on observing your gait. In coming from behind the shelter or from the seat after we have opened the doors, we may not be able to see your approach. Yes, there are those for whom a kneeler would be obvious, but asking for a kneeler after using the steps seems ass backwards. Putting a foot on the first step and not moving can work sometimes, especially if accompanied by a glare of disdain. The sense of entitlement I pick up on, however, does tend to make me pause sometimes in lowering the stairs. The quickest verbal command to get the steps to descend is a "thank you." Veteran riding seniors know to say thank you as they reach the stairway, and just like magic, the steps go down. Condescension not required for lowering or ascension—just ask any angel.

Another secret for getting what you need from the bus driver is to come to the front door if your stop got passed up. The button by the back doors sometimes does not register on our dash board and does not work as regularly as the chime cord by the windows. Being able to hear the bell is also a plus. Even if your volume is low, taking off one bud lets the driver know you can hear him/her talking. This courtesy has been lost on most folks.

Screaming or yelling may work, but a quick move to the front at the first safe place past the zone is better; if safe, we will lower the steps so you can get out not far from the previous bus stop. We are allowed to do this per safety rule but not out the back door. Late rings with a demand from the back steps do not usually result in an open door; coming to the front, however, does. We can see if a cyclist or skater is approaching, and we have better control over the doors. The pause or delay in stepping down the back stairs creates extra seconds of time that could mean a collision upon stepping down versus a safely-lowered kneeler up by the next crosswalk at the front door. We can also move the bus nose closer to the curb than at the back.

Another trick I make sure my student in line training understands is to use the front door/rear door toggle in front of the door dial. By delaying the front door from opening and opening only the rear first, migration of souls sets in, and the slow exiting senior has a chance to make it to the front steps before those on the sidewalk bulldoze up the steps. This also saves on the call to "move back!"

"Coming out!" Is a helpful verbal cue, but if you let us know where you plan to get off when you board, and we can see that you need extra time, we can delay opening the front door so you don't get the *bum rush* by those on the sidewalk. This federal ADA law (Americans Disability Act) protects you when you depart. *Help us help you!* I enjoy protecting your right to step down first, but if I don't know when you are getting off, those extra precious seconds are lost upon folks who bum rush up the stairs from the curb. Let me help you by requesting your stop, so I can put a request to a face and see where you are going to sit when you board.

Humility and redress with the appellation, "operator", does work better for getting what you need when you have to get off. Two golden words, "thank you," help preserve the Zen when coming to the front door for special requests.

# FLIP-UP SEATS

Just in front of the middoors are seats which can be flipped up so a wheel chair can be locked in place on the floor and not block the aisle. On some coaches, the hook underneath the seat pad is extremely difficult to unlock. It requires a punch on the seat top above the underside hook and then a definite, but very subtle pull-down away from the seat back and towards the floor. As many passengers are willing to assist in flipping the seats up for a boarding wheelchair patron, their ability to locate the seat hook lever often ends in frustration, or if found, still ends without a flip-up because they don't pull down and away. Having my interior view mirror correctly angled, I can come to the rescue by demonstrating the correct way to flip up the seats. This adds one more passenger to the list of those who can help open up this space in the future and keeps a vested interest in departing as soon as possible from the bus stop.

On our older coaches, the forward-facing seats do drop down randomly, much to the surprise of anyone not anticipating a loud noise. Muni has marked these chairs and now has them in the locked and upright position. This is for safety. I now make sure I hear the click when the chair is secure. I can also ask if boarders are ready. Usually, they give a sign that they are locked in and secure. If I cannot see them because the aisle is full, I have learned the hard way that I must ask first, before starting.

I must also be patient with food carts, strollers, and any other odd-sized object a passenger may be carrying. The forward-facing seats now locked upright, really help with strollers and food carts. If they aren't locked properly, I will hear the sound of apples and oranges thumping and rolling on the floor, or the sound of a paper bag ripping and falling on the floor. When a body falls, we usually can't hear it unless a cane is involved. The saving grace is that when the bus is packed, the other human bodies do act as a nice cushion against a full, on-the-floor knock-down. Wheelchair users almost always holler if they are not locked in when I start rolling. "We're rolling!" is a command I usually issue if I cannot see everyone.

But a rule that seems to be lost on most boarding passengers is that, if they are holding an oversized object like a surf board or a floor lamp, permission must be secured by the operator to bring the item on board. The sense of entitlement that would-be passengers have, without questioning safety issues, is astonishing. I have allowed a glass-topped end table on board, as well as a floor lamp with light bulb and torchiere. But all of these fragile items were after the seats were flipped up, and the coach was relatively empty. The passengers were also counseled on proper etiquette before boarding. *It is not a given that you can use Muni as a moving company.*

No, you can't bring a red metal gas can on board, even if you say it is empty. No, car batteries are not allowed. Muni is not AAA, and we are not a moving company, though I can think of instances where this has nearly been true. It is a bummer if your car is out of gas or needs a jump, but a bus is not the vehicle to get gas or a new battery and bring it back to your car. It's just the lack of willingness to request a ride that is usually accompanied by a lack of judgment about what Muni is and is not. Boa constrictors, birds of paradise, all things great and small, board with their owners. I can't think of a single species that has not been claimed as a pet or guide animal.

In any case, the flip-up seats have saved many a tense situation in passenger relations if I have the wherewithal to flip up the seats for an oversized object. And the gratitude I receive feels good. I do like the idea that things get carried and brought on that no other transit agency would allow. The fact that you can find a great lamp or piece of furniture to bring home without a cab or moving truck by taking the bus, is a very rare and precious commodity that makes San Francisco unique. I would hate to be a part of an end to that perception. Keeping Zen is keeping the flip seats available for whatever may come my way.

# AVENUES OR STREETS?

My friends always ask me about what line I am driving. Then they ask about the F Streetcar line on Market Street. The railway has a number of historic streetcars from around the world, and they have been restored and repainted in colors from cities such as Melbourne, Philadelphia, Milan, and Kansas City. It is a wonder to see these multicolored street cars make their proud way down Market Street.

Like most streets in San Francisco, we just use the name of the street when we converse. So we refer to our promenade thoroughfare as Market. We rarely add the word *street*, except when directing those to our numbered avenues or streets. The avenues are out west by Ocean Beach, the Sunset, and the Richmond, and streets are downtown, SOMA, or in the Mission.

Curiously, few visitors or first-timers are aware of this. The question, "Do you go to 25th?" can be answered incorrectly by just saying yes or no. If on a crosstown bus, we must get avenue or street from the visitor. If leaving downtown, we must also ask, "Do you mean street or avenue?"

Twenty-fifth Avenue is nowhere near 25th Street, so by answering yes, someone can be misled by several miles from their intended destination by only giving the number without street or avenue. This can add over an hour to transit time. Directions are critical when talking on the phone or writing information down on a piece of paper. Most of those who fail to meet a friend or get to a new residence or employer are missing a key piece of information when they obtain it over the phone.

The next problem is not having the phone number to recall the person who gave the directions. Or not carrying a charged cell phone to make another call while on the bus. If I am driving in a peak direction, I refer the person asking questions to another person on the bus if it looks like he/she doesn't have all the information needed to arrive at the intended destination. After two attempts, I have to disengage. Not being sure of a stop request can be a distraction while I drive, so I have to be careful that I am still friendly in ending the conversation. Sometimes, a lack of understanding about safety creates a discourteous impression, and I have to keep my Zen if I am to stay out of trouble.

Make sure you get the cross street when asking for directions. Make sure the other party is not giving you a side street as a cross street; a side street is only one or two blocks long. Many of us are unfamiliar with these side streets or alleyways. I would love a driver test about the streets of San Francisco, and I know certain shuttle companies do have this. I would like to see a tourist question guide added to our training. "Do you go to BART?" "Do you go to Fisherman's Wharf?" "Do you go to the train station?" Inevitably, the time and place where these questions are asked are as predictable as the tides. (Good idea for my next book!)

Keeping the Zen in transit means having the cross street down before boarding a crowded bus. Having the connection point and knowing the interval or headway between bus lines also helps to reduce lost time between transfers. The transfer cost between modes and agencies is a primary reason for loss of ridership to the automobile.

# ISLANDS AND CURBS

On Market Street, there are two places on a block to catch or pick up a bus. If you have your *Incredibles* superhero costume tights on, you should know the newer ETI Skoda trolleys weigh about ten tons sans passengers, so be careful you don't pull your back muscles when you catch the approaching bus and lift it above your head. For most of us mortals, however, taking a bus on the curb or on an island is recommended.

The curb stops are located midblock, and the island stops are near an intersection by a corner or a cross street. Unbeknownst to most San

Franciscans, however, is a method to the madness of these two sets of stops. Island stops outbound take you south of Golden Gate Park to the Sunset, and curb stops, located midblock, take you outbound to the Richmond, which is north of Golden Gate Park. So, if you were heading to Cliff House, Lake Street, Land's End, or the Legion of Honor, you would move to a curb stop after exiting a BART station under Market Street. These destinations are north of Golden Gate Park.

The 5, 21, 31, and 38 all go to the residential area (the Richmond) between the Presidio and Golden Gate Park. The 6, 7, 7R, 9, 9R all stop on the outbound islands at an intersection on Market and take you to the Inner Sunset or points south of Golden Gate Park.

The 9 and 9R service the Bayview/Visitacion Valley area by diverging off of Market just before Van Ness. The point is that all these buses eventually leave Market Street, some sooner than others. The 1 never actually touches Market and is a good escape from downtown from Embarcadero BART if a special event is taking place on Market, such as a parade or protest. And we have tons of them.

The single aspect that puts San Francisco in the number one spot of living up to the phrase, "The City That Knows How," is our flexibility about street closures and reroutes for ongoing and recurring special events. I don't believe any other major metropolitan area has as many street fairs, farmer's markets, special events, and parades as we do. The President was here again last week. Our *Governator* would also have meetings at a downtown hotel. The Defense Secretary was here to sign off on his Halliburton millions, and the list goes on for motorcade delays like marathons and races, the Bay to Breakers before Memorial Day weekend, various street fairs, Juneteenth, The Cherry Blossom Festival, Chinese New Year, The Dragon Parade, Freedom Parade, Dore Alley, Castro, Folsom, Fillmore Jazz, and Union Street fairs, North Beach art shows, art crawls, bike races, Fleet Week, and on and on. All have alerts and special reroutes and delays.

The only other thing to talk about is the islands on Market. If you look carefully at the Muni bus stop pole, the sign says *weekdays only* for certain buses. Those looking for express service would do well to read this information.

These flag poles have information most bus companies don't provide at a stop. Inbound versus outbound is important for express service, as an X bus only works inbound in the morning and outbound in the afternoon. The exception is the 82X, which can be picked up on Main Street by the Federal Reserve building both in the morning and afternoon. This express is a loop that operates like a crosstown express loop during the morning and evening rush.

Charter and tour buses ferrying workers to the peninsula have filled in this lack of loop service not provided by city transit. A series of loops in the city would reduce the pickup and zone sharing at bus stops made by the shuttles, but this costly change in the past has not been justified by the riding numbers. The new density created by all the towers and buildings going up, however, may need a serious revisit on this possibility. Muni could run crosstown loops to connect with peninsula shuttles or Cal Train.

The express signs add the terms *am* or *pm*, and this is as important as the *weekdays* reminder! Keeping my Zen on, I try to collect these lost puppies, but sometimes it isn't possible to capture everyone. Woe betides the operator on the F line on the weekend and good luck as an information specialist! This is why I love just driving the locals around on a Potrero barn coach.

# CRUNCH ZONE

I picked up a man in a wheelchair near downtown at Third Street outbound and was amazed at how smooth and fast he boarded and locked in. I could tell he was a regular rider. Instinctively, I knew he was going to get off at 16th and Mission, and sure enough, when I asked, he stated he was going to 16th. I told him I was glad to have a regular rider who knew how to ride Muni. He talked about his learning curve on how to work the flip-up seats and about where to get on and get off. If there was any heartfelt strength of purpose to distribute this book to the masses, it is not about the money or the power or the vanity of being an author, but to get out the wisdom about how to ride, so that the bus system moves faster and creates fewer headaches for those getting around. Nowhere is this wisdom needed more than in the crunch zone.

At first, I wanted to call this chapter, "Crunch Time," as it pertains to the operation of a bus from 3:30 p.m. to 6:30 p.m. However, the pattern of movement between two stops was as predictable as the time frame, and I realized a more accurate description of gridlock was in certain zones between stops. And the idea for this chapter was born in the conversation with this wheelchair rider as he glided away from downtown with me in a calm, roomy coach. If there is an opposite to being in the Zen zone, this chapter is it. I found out he wanted to go up Van Ness to Geary, but was passing up the transfer point by four blocks. Now I know why. He was avoiding having to board a trolley in the crunch zone.

On the 14 Mission, the crunch zone exists between 16th Street and 7th inbound in the morning, and Fourth and Eleventh outbound in the afternoon. The sequence of events is so repetitive and coincidental that one could plot a graph of predictability on an actuarial table for an insurance company. Come to think of it, the City of San Francisco *is* an insurance company. I don't know how this would help with claims, but like this man who was on my coach, avoiding the problem areas makes for an easy ride, even if it means traveling beyond the shortest distance between two points.

Indeed, I found this out as a rider in my thirties, new to the city in the 1980s. In getting to my warehouse in Hunter's Point and Bayview from the Tenderloin, the shortest route was the 19 Polk. But the fastest way was to go inbound on the Geary bus to catch a 15 Third. I made a large checkmark inbound to outbound rather than go crosstown direct.

And this is true of the crunch zones between the 49 Van Ness and the 14 Mission. Especially if you are in a wheelchair, carrying a large cumbersome object, or using a grocery cart. Also, if you have difficulty in getting up the stairs or need a seat right by the door, oddly enough, the best offense is the defense of traveling beyond the closest stop to your destination. This means backtracking to board where the bus is less crowded. Many riders have learned this about getting on a train under Market Street.

The crunch zone for the 49 Van Ness builds as the bus moves inbound to the streets numbered in the teens until 14th Street, where room runs out and there is nowhere to sit or stand. Cyclists, walkers, and those receiving food bank items filling a grocery cart all wait in the crunch zone. If there are two coaches bunched together, usually everything is fine. But if there are gaps between buses, a pass-up frequently prevents crowding problems.

On the 49 line, the crunch zone exists between 16th Street and Eddy inbound, and from O'Farrell to Otis outbound. Load factors and working leaders influence the zone by making it longer or shorter, but in general, I have to make sure people boarding do the right thing by sitting or standing in such a way as to prevent fights or arguments at the following stops. Crunch zones also lie in the Inner Mission between 18th and 30th outbound in the p.m. Also, before 24th St. BART inbound in the morning commute. People listen better before their space is threatened.

This is a golden key to the crunch zone. I, too, have a better vibe and tone if I ask someone to move before the crunch zone hits. And when those who have moved see that those I next pick up need the first two seats, the message has hit home in a way that is not threatening or defensive. Score one for the Zen!

# APC COACH

If I see the call light on when I board my coach in the morning, or I see the radio programmed with another run and line, I reprogram the radio with my line and run and call Central for a radio and time check. The response time from Central also gives me a sense of how busy they are. Especially when I have been detailed to another coach in the yard because mine was given away, or had problems, and the coach I am leaving with is different than the one originally assigned me by the yard starter. My run may require an APC coach. This is a coach with infrared laser beams by the doors to count how many passengers are boarding. APC stands for automated passenger counter.

The computer registers every time we open the door and for how long. It also captures and records dwell time in the zone. APC coaches, marked on the front windscreen, count how many board and depart at each stop. You can see if a coach has this by looking at those red lights and reflectors at the top of a stairwell by the doors.

The traffic checkers were on my 22 bus all last week. They were riding to verify that the APC laser beams were accurately tallying the passenger count on and off my bus. After a long school trip, there they were, still on board near the rear door. We have less than ten checkers left on hire. Most agencies our size have a department of over twenty checkers. Federal money mandates that we have payroll for such a staff. The human element of keeping tabs on counting passengers is more accurate than a laser beam that may miscount. A youth can spin on the rear pole and cause a high on/off count when no such traffic exists.

There are so many variables that can affect the passenger count. I am amazed that anyone could make heads or tails of the mass of numbers that must be generated by coach counters. I can't speak for other operators, but when I get an APC coach, I definitely do all I can to fill that puppy up.

If I get too close to my leader, I will have an empty bus, and my run may not get filled on the next sign-up. I want the data to reflect a busy and crowded day and show that I come to work to do just that. I'd be damned if, on the day I get an APC coach, I have no one in the aisle! Oh look, my leader just broke down, and now my bus is packed. Eat *that* in your data crunch! Keeping busy and keeping rolling on down the line is keeping the Zen for me in San Francisco transit.

# OVER THERE

"Should I wait for the bus over there?" Silence. No response from the operator. Can he or she see where you're talking about? Does the operator see your finger and guess which corner or direction you are pointing toward? This question usually is not answered. If I am in the middle of something like the crosswalk, the turning car, the waiting truck, the cyclist approaching, I don't have a second set of eyes to find the direction or spot you are pointing to.

As soon as I can qualify and describe a landmark in the big view in front of the bus, things become clearer. If inside the coach, I must come to rest before I can safely give you the answer you need. I have to look at this from a point of view other than my own. I can stop and open the door where you are standing in the aisle behind me, offer a suggestion based on the scene in front, and wait for you to decide what to do. I need the space to stop, look, and listen.

I have tried to simplify this by saying, "Yes." But nine out of ten times, the question is repeated again. "You mean over there?" "Yes." "Going that way?" "Yes." "Or is it that way?" "No."

Third time is not a charm. The answer is yes and the case is closed. And so is the door. "Hold on, we're rolling!" I may not have eyes in the back of my head if my interior rear view mirror is above or below where your finger is pointing; and even then, just what part of the finger *am* I supposed to look at? The one finger that always leaves no doubt—the middle finger sticking straight up in the air!

# FLAT TIRE

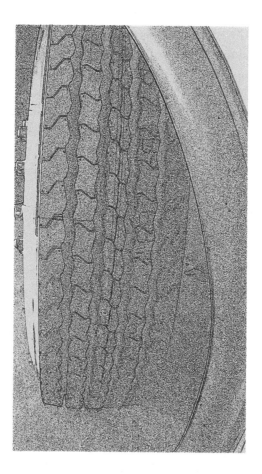

The wheels on the bus go round and round all through the town, except for when there is a construction detour, or another patch job in the making from the Water Department, or PG&E, the utility company! The wheels go round and round, even if the tire tread doesn't. But you would never know, because the only thing rougher than the tires are the street surfaces.

Only once did my bus get a flat. An actual flat tire with an air leak where the rubber scrunches down on the street. There was a house under construction, and I ran over a nail. A huge nail. The bus tires cost like 800 dollars apiece and have 27 mm thickness. I did not believe they would ever spring a leak. I called for the tire man who came out and fixed the flat. This was the only time I had to make a road call for a flat tire.

When we put flat tire on our defect card, it doesn't mean we have a tire out of air. Flat tire means our tread has worn unevenly, and when we take our coach up to twenty miles per hour, we hear the drums along the Mohawk. A "thump-thump," as the worn or flat portion of the tread goes round and round. Only on a newly-surfaced street can we tell that we have a flat tire. But there is not too much worry about here. When streets are resurfaced, they are only paved a block at a time and in small sections. This factor hides the brand new tire with a sometime defective tread that has been put on a bus.

Perfectly round tires are replaced with new, scalloped ones. This is an improvement from tire treads that would separate on a hot day when we turned the front wheel. Those were tires probably were labelled as new, but it is obvious when recapped tires are used instead. You can see the separation line on the cap versus a brand new tire. I will pull in with a perfectly good bus, and the shop man in the tower puts up a chit for new tires. Resistance is futile. If I pull in with flat tire on the defect card, I get a look of disdain, as if I am doing something wrong. New tires seem to be inspected not when they are put on a bus, but when I pull in and turn the front wheel to inspect the tread at the tower. The fault, dear Brutus, is not with the shop, but with the quality of the tires shipped to us as *new*.

The shop man in the tower makes it very clear what is and is not a safety significant defect in the tire, and any balding tire showing through to the inner nylon mesh is removed per state and federal law. We cannot have a shallow tread of less than 4/32 of an inch on the front wheels. They are rotated to the back, inner rear wheels on the long coaches.

I have been asked by my editor to clarify terms used in this book, such as the term, "safety significant." The October 8, 1999 memo of a previous administration is often cited when describing safety significant defects;

we are to report them immediately and take the coach out of service. But interestingly, the letter never states what they are. And so now, right here, right now—just like Jesus Jones—I get to be the unacknowledged legislator of "safety significant" as fresh, untainted eyes read this page. One definition of safety significant is something for which parts are available!

Seriously though, I turn to what our protocol is for using the priority button on our radio. A priority is any threat to life or limb of anyone on or around the bus. A door that opens on a moving trolley or train is, therefore, a safety significant risk. A burned-out trim light or a dirty vent panel is not. A new tire with a blemish in the tread may not be safety significant if the tread is maintained at 4/32 of an inch. This is where the defect card, to be filled out and turned-in at the tower as we pull in, comes into play. If, on a tire, I mark "shimmy" and "hard-steering," the shop responds immediately. If I mark "flat tire," nothing may happen, especially if I don't mark which specific tire has the drums along the Mohawk sound.

The only thing worse than a flat tire on a bus is one on a bike. But the good news is that every bus has a bike rack to take you back to the shop for a new one or just some air. I always give you a free ride if your bike gets a flat on the street. Also, just to let you motorists or car people know, if your car is in the shop, I'll break off a long one for you for taking mass transit for the first time. The first ride is free!

# HOT LUNCH

As I walk to my corner coffee shop at zero dark thirty in the morning, I see another splayed design of "ejecta" on the sidewalk from someone's drinking spree last night. At least this "hot lunch" occurred outside of the aisle and stairwell of a Muni bus. When someone pukes on the bus, we can pull the coach in with what we call a hot lunch. This means my follower will have a double load and less time for break at the next terminal. I believe this is why God invented newspaper, for travelers who make messes on and in the bus.

Newspapers wedged between the seats or crumpled on the floor make for a quick and convenient remedy for keeping the bus in regular service. I usually don't throw newspapers off the bus when it is raining or if I am working weekends or when school is out. I may need the paper to clean rain-soaked floors or mirrors or clean up any other mess of fluids left on the bus. The art becomes using the paper so as to not need gloves to touch any part of the blood, feces, or vomit. And yes, it would be nice if we had bathrooms with hot water at the end of the line. Soap and towels are the luxury of a tour bus operator, I guess.

Teen girls are the number one offender when it comes to puking on the bus. Hopefully, I can spot them before they get on. Usually, their girlfriends are helping them walk up to the steps. I ask, "Hey, why don't you wait a few more minutes and get your balance first?" or "How far are you going?" If they show no sign of listening, or no intention to step off and wait for the next wave of heaving, then I say, "Okay, sit near the door and let me know when you have an emergency!" At least this minimizes any damage to the floor of the aisle. If the steps do get hit, it can be dangerous, depending on the type of vomit.

You know, you have your clear, almost invisible kind. This dissipates quickly and has no odor. It can provide extra traction as it hardens or dissolves and is mostly from stomach acids and esophageal mucus. It's a bonus if the teenage girl hasn't eaten. Then, of course, there are the slippery, half-digested refried beans. The rice can provide traction, and the birds do like this if it makes it to the sidewalk. If she is with guys, they usually dump her and get off the bus early. They laugh and think it's funny. Some *friends,* indeed. And if she's with a girlfriend, the point seems to be to get home as fast as possible. So even though she is being "helped," am I really doing my duty by not calling for help? Should this be an ambulance call? The possibility of alcohol poisoning exists, and use of a stomach pump may be in order. Perhaps I could let them stay at the stop and call the police. The balance of a major family event stands on the tips of my fingers with a call to Central Control.

Will there be a hospital and ambulance bill? Is this just another weekend learning experience for two friends? Should I intervene or get on with moving my passengers down the road? Being a night-time driver on the Mission requires making snap judgment calls between an emergency treatment or a quick, first-aid remedy. I usually go with first-aid: Have them step off the rear door before the heaves get too bad, and then use the newspapers to sop up the goo and to keep the walking tread dry. Then a scoop-up of the papers at the next terminal or a swing-by at a convenient trash can.

It can be a drag if the person puking doesn't want to exit and continues to heave while sitting on the bus. The other passengers become uncomfortable if I don't do something. I cannot ignore sick people on the bus, unless they are way in the back, and the bus is full, and no one comes forward. Fortunately, the empty stomach is what causes the problem in the first place, so there is not too much to clean up. Hopefully. The insanity of getting on the bus to go home is impossible to override if the person sick is with a group of "friends." As with everything else, going with the flow keeps us moving.

So if you are riding on or driving the 14 Mission after dark, especially on weekends, make sure you have a copy of the morning edition!

# CAR CLEANERS

I am sure these coworkers have stories to tell. I can only imagine what sorts of things they have had to pick up, wipe up, or mop up in their day. If there be any sequel to this missive, I am sure the experiences of graffiti cleaners, floor sweepers, or those who pick up the trash will produce some interesting tales.

Dipping dots and chicken bones are not high on my list of favorites. Neither are the empty cups of mixed iced coffee or smoothies. Open containers of soda or beer are the biggest bummer, especially when not completely empty. They can fall from the small platform next to the rear seats and get kicked around on the floor, sending a trail of sticky fluid halfway up the aisle.

We are supposed to do a walk-through to the back of the coach at every terminal. This is important to see if anyone has left anything by his/her seat. I once found a paperback with 500 dollars in an envelope acting as a bookmark on the number 6 Line at 14th Avenue and Quintara. I put the book up on the dash before I left the outbound terminal. Sure enough, when I started back down the hill to 9th and Judah two young men rushed into the street in front of the bus and started screaming and waving for me to stop. This was on a dark, moonless night. I opened the door and held the book up in my hand.

"Envelope? What envelope?" I couldn't resist. "The money is still there." They were relieved to say the least. It was rent money. Paying rent by cash in San Francisco is common on grandfathered, long-term leases, but it can add to drama and problems when the money disappears.

The other big-ticket item was a laptop computer. Fortunately, there was a name and phone number in the case, and I was able to call the owner immediately. She was so happy to get that one back. With cell phones, too, I can usually find a recently-called number belonging to a friend of the owner and let them know I have it. In all these cases, I call Central Control as soon as I know I have something, and when the passenger calls the 3-1-1 information number Central lets them know when my bus will pass back in their direction. They are so happy to see me coming. This is probably the nicest feedback and recognition I receive at this job. It can happen so quickly and simply, and all I have to do is make a sweep of the coach at the end of the line.

Not only can this result in the most rewarding gratitude from a passenger, but it can prevent a nasty, sticky mosaic of soda or beer in the aisle from the back seat to the front seats. Ice cream on a hot day really creates a sticky hazard when it is stuck to the floor like crazy glue. Once, a little girl dropped her ice cream ball atop her cone right onto the lap of a nicely-dressed woman going to a job interview. Words to the wise: When going to an interview, take a cab. Or bring some detergent wipes, just in case.

And then there is the full cup of joe without a lid. One person tripped up the steps and doused my shirt with coffee. Oh well, at least the color matched the uniform! We are allowed to go out of service for up to two hours to get a new shirt, but I kept on going. Here was the opportunity to state why bringing drinks on the bus was not a good idea, and it stuck.

Newly-hired car cleaners have been present on the track and in my coach before I pull out in the morning. I see them applying the finishing touches on the windows and cockpit. The floor is freshly-mopped. The bus is spotless. A passenger on my first trip noted the wet floors as a potential hazard. I grinned. Enjoy it while it lasts!

# SAFE DRIVER AWARD

Next time you see an operator wearing a safe driver patch, ask yourself what it reminds you of. Is it a nuclear or biological warfare hazard symbol? Perhaps it is a design not unlike the fallout shelter signs of the fifties and sixties. No, this is the safe driving award patch for a transit operator who has had no accident for 365 consecutive days. The cost of this patch could be about twenty-five cents (maybe even a dollar for inflation), but the *price* is incredibly high!

As any transit rider can attest, the odds of making this happen are incredible. All one has to do is ride in the seat across from the cockpit in a trolley for just ten blocks to see the continuous threats and trespassing from pedestrians, skaters, cyclists, motorists, and delivery trucks. And to extrapolate this continuous, hyper-aware adrenaline state day after day, month after month, for up to a twelve-hour range for a day shift, the elevation to heroic status of a San Francisco Transit Operator is not that boastful or unrealistic.

But guess what? The one-year patches were eliminated. Perhaps the arm's length of patches on the shirt sleeve or Ike jacket was tacky looking. I don't understand why this needed to be taken back. It reminds me of the new rule to allow cell phones on airplanes or to stop charging for parking meters on Sunday. It feels like a step backward in progress.

Thanks to the vilification of operators as "Fat Cats" in the news during the economic downturn of the late 2000s, and a misapplied label of a nontaxable, health benefits check (described as a "bonus" check), our annual trust fund check before Christmas was removed. And no more automatic cost-of-living increases of twenty-five cents per hour twice a year, per city charter, to keep up with inflation. No more benefits check, no more annual safe-driving award patch. Ouch. And, of course, the politician doing this service work is no longer in office. So now, my purpose in writing this second missive is to shift sentiment back in a positive way so that we can all be proud of taking a bus.

But many riders I talk to are glad that we operators, as a class, have been brought back down to earth in our job description and pay. These are the *lucky to have a job* group. Call in sick within two days of a new sign-up, and you may lose your run. You are put on the extra board, or you are kicked down to last place in days off on an owl run, as an example.

If you work a seventh day straight, you don't get overtime if, during any day of the second week, you miss a day of work. These are the inefficient work rules taken away by a voter-mandated proposition G. Lately, however, this tide has shifted to where many riders say we don't make enough. We have gone for over five years without a raise and had a sick-out protest over conditions offered in the next contract.

If someone was caught in traffic coming over the bridge, their run would be given to a stand-by, on-report operator, and they would be detailed on the next open run. They did not need to call if they were driving and in traffic. This situation was portrayed as not being able to show up for work and was eliminated years ago in proposition M. But for years and years after M's passage, the anger of not showing up and not calling in was used as a weapon against the supposition that we had it too good. The point being, our rules were set up for minimal drama and with the understanding that we would not strike if our wages kept up with inflation.

I heard of the tumult in Wisconsin and other such previously "blue" states that the halcyon days of benefits and pay are over. Indeed, most government workers' benefits now exceed those in the private sector, except when they don't. As witnessed by the huge bonus checks received by those working in technology, I certainly do not begrudge this. The spotlight has shifted off of us as a class, and onto the tech workers. Most vivid is the example of Muni being blocked by the tour buses taking tech employees to work in the morning or home in the evening using our bus stops.

Once again, the idea being pushed is that income inequality is awful, and that penalties should apply, such as a use fee for a tour coach to use a Muni bus stop. Rather than see a rising tide lifting all boats, the lock and dam should be shut until all the dinghy's leaks can be plugged.

But I digress. I still don't see why a safe driver patch that is such a challenge to obtain and costs so little should be canceled. As a former Boy Scout who loves trading and collecting patches, it wasn't the five years of no raise or the removal of the three thousand dollars of benefits per year caused by a voter-mandated change in our city charter. The kick in the solar plexus was the removal of the annual safe driver award patch.

Lest you get the feeling that I enjoy being the victim, let me state for the record that, while I do relish the familiarity of this *victim* energy, I do love the elation that comes from meeting a seemingly impossible goal without any fanfare or regal ceremony. It is so familiar to get into the blame mode or the *look what they are doing to us* mode, but this option offers no solution.

When we are done with our work, we are done. If we have made plans outside of drive time, this precious commodity of our personal time can't be *bought* for any price! Though it sure seems like the boat has a slow leak. Is that hissing sound coming from the parking brake? How much air are we supposed to maintain in pounds-per-square-inch per minute with the lines open or with the service brake applied? The only air leak is the hot air from politicians taking away wages or benefits.

There was only one simple message for this patch design—the image and symbol of the safe driver award. As for the the Nobel Peace Prize, the Medal of Honor, the Distinguished Service Cross, and the Silver Star, the Safe Driver Award should be ranked alongside them. Gallantry in action or wounds suffered in combat—these seem like just another day behind the wheel of a city bus.

Then there are those who pass the twenty-year mark. These are the true masters of the Zen. Indeed, most of my failures and accidents have caused me to be a better operator, but I still have not made it to ten years of safe driving, even though I have been at the job for sixteen years. This book is written for those like me whose annual safe driving does not match years of service. Those first few years were hum-dingers!

Cue dead roll music: flute, drum and fife, bagpipe, and hell, a bugle corps! Keeping Zen should be that state of bliss, a way or a path of success from where, when we look back after having climbed the mountain, the view is fantastic.

But wait, does this mean that we are trudging in pain all the way up the rickety bridge or rocky trail? What kind of a life is that? No, the secret of Zen should be with us at all times. We need to know that it is always available to us, and we can see the vantage point, even though we are not yet there. The spiritual quest can be found on any yoga floor, on any bus. No longer isolated as a pod person in a separate machine, we are together on the bus. No wonder the little ones love the bus!

# OPEN RUN

It took me several years to learn this term. I found out about it after overhearing Central Control responding to a street operations inspector on the corner inquiring about a run number. "That run is a not-out," was the response to a blank space in the headway between buses.

The rules are as clear as the black and white numbers of a railway timetable about our leaving times, minutes between coaches, and checkpoints along the way. The only thing is we have no printed timetables. (I have to admit, I added that last sentence to make it sound more dramatic.) The truth is it really doesn't matter that we have no published timetables. And as the street inspectors have been removed from Chestnut and Fillmore, Sutter and Fillmore, 16th and Bryant, Third and 20th, and other places, such as Potrero and 16th and Kansas and 17th, it makes little difference anyway.

Just like the prelude to an elimination of a line, cutting service reduces ridership and lessens the attraction of riding a bus in the first place. At some point, cost reduction becomes self-fulfilling, and so we, too, as a class of operators, become adjusted to the new realities of having a bus or buses missing in front of us. This adds to pass-ups due to full coaches and leads to the missive, "to throw out the schedule" when operating a coach on the line.

I heard a lot about cost-cutting four or five years ago. Now, I hear a sarcastic and condescending tone about making up a schedule and making up stops. With an on-time performance of around 60 percent, I just laugh at this comment. If we had a level of punctuality of over 85 percent, then I could see the point in running on time. But as it is, a difference of 62 versus 63 percent makes no visible difference.

The hard part of all of this is guessing how to adjust headway and speed, not knowing what kind of a day we are going to have. The standard response is to make all stops until the coach fills up, and then begin skipping stops. I object to this sometimes because the folks in the middle of the line get passed up more frequently and get lousy service. This becomes more apparent during special events, when large crowds wait along avenues by Golden Gate Park after the Bay to Breakers race or the Barely Bluegrass festival.

Some coworkers disagree with me about letting passengers know that there is a bus missing in front of or behind me. I believe knowledge is power, and most of my riders are glad to be informed. But I do get the drift that many of my coworkers abide by an "ignorance is bliss" mode.

In any case, knowing that I don't have a leader by an open run helps me in knowing what to expect. I am not one to be a cry-baby to the dispatcher or the union about how bad I have it with an open run. I have seen others attempt this drama to little effect. Big mouths and cry-babies run hot, and so I have to dial it down when it comes to what headway I am experiencing.

I love it when I am away for a week, and I hear complaints from my regulars or the operator doing my run. What was once a quiet and uncomplaining operator on a run becomes an "O my god" when I am away. I always love hearing about how bad it was when I was off, and an open run leader is no exception. Interestingly, when I come back from vacation, the open run in front of me magically gets filled. There may be a reward in heaven for me working without a leader, but I do get a taste of this when I come back from being away for a while.

Thank you for riding!

# FOLLOW MY LEADER

*It seems like a quiet Friday today*, I think to myself. The bus has several seats open; no one is standing in the aisle. The bus is most definitely in the Zen zone, even though we are halfway through the trip in the middle of the line. How can this be? The answer is usually right in front of your eyes. If you scan through the windscreen (windshield) a few blocks ahead, you should see the tail lights of another trolley running late or on *my* time. Until recently, I thought this was a form of heaven on earth, a time to make good money without the fight over a seat or space.

But with GPS, DVAS, and computer technology on the bus recording every door opening and every stop, I realized I must adapt more acutely to this record-keeping by observing the one block spacing rule. Following too closely is a no-no that can generate a citation from an officer of the law if contact is made at a stop sign or light when rear-ended by another car. As bus drivers, we can also receive a written warning based upon the actions of our operation if we stay too close to our leader—the bus in front of us. If the DVAS clock display is off by six minutes, I must call Central for a time check.

The problem for me is mental. I am in such a runner's mode, having been trained on the Mission lines without a leader, that I am preprogrammed to shave every unnecessary second off of dwell time in the zone. I can move up four minutes without leaving early from the terminal. And when Central gives me orders to move up four, I have to signal this to my follower so as not to create a hole in time behind me.

Here's a case in point on the 49 Van Ness. There was no help from the 47s. Four minutes would not have made a difference, as three coaches of help from the 47 were not there. By checking door movements, it was obvious I was skipping stops. And by leaving late, it could be seen that I was "playing games." But none of this had anything to do with my desire to get down Van Ness without incident. The written record of passenger complaints against me was actually about overcrowding and lack of other service to Caltrain on the 47.

Letters to the editor in local news press reflect the same angry sentiment we bus drivers have when we get disciplined with days off without pay. The Bus Rapid Transit Lane is trumpeted as a plan to speed the commute but is of little value in the here and now when buses are missing, and angry commuters see a full 49 passing them up.

So "follow my leader" is usually a sign that my leader is full and needs help. If I follow too closely, pass-ups can result in late runners or confusion about which bus to board if intenders have been waiting too long and clog the doors of the bus in front. The natural beat that occurs between buses with a regular interval of seven minutes gets ruined when bunching occurs.

So, what I have learned is to disable my move-up mode, and hold doors open at an empty zone to keep spacing at more than just a block. I have found that three blocks is usually the shortest space required to keep things flowing. If I have a bus behind me catching up and getting too close, I must not let this force me to speed up. These subtle pressures can build and lead to a write-up. So, even though technology is providing the black and white data for discipline, key factors like other bus lines or DVAS clock time missing or being off by several minutes render an accurate or predictable snapshot impossible.

# RESTRICTED MODE

This devilish mode is found in the morning when someone turns on the coach in neutral; it's a bummer when you need to pull out on track four. Nowhere can the ghosts inhabiting some buses be found more frequently than in the flashing red light on the dash that notes propulsion down or reduced performance. On some coaches, it is the horn or the windshield wipers that go on or off unexpectedly; on others, the problem can be in the vents or in trying to open the driver's window.

One bus has its spiritual signature on the back window emergency lever. It won't lock, and if you try to seal the window, the whole window comes out. As experienced operators, we eventually get a working knowledge of what quirk each coach has. We can log a diary of the coach number and what the "defect" is, so that when we get the coach again, we already know what to do or not to do. Over time, we don't even need to look at our diary; we already know instinctively.

Restricted mode is tough because it can change from coach to coach and from time to time. All we can do is try to follow the manufacturer's specifications to the letter and hope we don't omit any step or procedure that might start the cascade all over again. For example, waiting a full two minutes with the coach turned off before we restart. (Needless to say, if stopped in a busy intersection, motorists may have other ideas about waiting a full two minutes while the bus is blocking traffic.) Turning on the bus when in neutral is a no-no for some, but on other coaches, it is required.

Leaving the heat or blowers on can create an energy drain that some buses won't tolerate when "waking up." Likewise, turning on the blower motors too soon after turning on the engine can also create payback complaints from the bus.

In the pre-op test before becoming an operator, the first line item action is addressing the coach. I literally greet my coaches before I board. If I fail to do this, I can quickly get into trouble. I do talk to my buses when I approach them from behind in the yard or from the front in the garage. If I am finely attuned, I can sense a problem as soon as I am assigned a coach by the yard starter. And of late, my intuition seems uncanny in its accuracy. If I am asleep in my awareness, however, I can get bitten by doors that won't close or a radio that doesn't work or a power drain that brings the bus to a halt. I try to coax them back to life, but if they fail me at an inopportune moment, I do happen to tell them a thing or two, like Sigourney Weaver as Ripley in the movie, *Aliens*.

The point of no return seems to be when I have tried to reset master control for a third time without success. I reach a point where no more tricks or clicks will bring the coach back to life. It is time to call for help. Imagine my shock when the radio won't transmit, especially if I happen to be in the middle of an intersection.

But my overhead power karma is good, and I usually can get out of a blocked situation fast. I always try to help another stuck operator to keep my matrix clear. Many such problems are those that never "stick" because of our fit spiritual condition. A good pre-op pays huge dividends on the road later in the day. I am always relieved when I find a problem on track four and not at Sansome and Sutter.

# UPPER YARD

At the Potrero trolley bus barn, we have two levels. Unlike the Presidio trolley barn (which has one level and a tricky pull-out from track one and a pull-out to Sutter) the Potrero barn has many lanes of challenging tracks. There is a horseshoe U-turn maneuver from tracks ten, eleven, and twelve that can lock up an articulated coach in the lower yard by the wash rack.

The upper yard has an S-curve maneuver from tracks thirty, thirty-one, and thirty-two to the street that also makes it difficult to prevent a lock-up or de-wiring. Not only is the far side curb clearance an issue with parked cars, but the traffic on 17th Street does not want to yield or be slowed by a pull-out coach. In the evening, the car parkers run the gauntlet of passing through the tire shop. Potrero has car parkers to speed parking and prevent blocking. This necessity becomes clear when many coaches pull in together in the evening after rush hour is over. The car parkers also insure coaches are left on park charge correctly and that accessories are turned off.

There was a brief time when the car parkers were eliminated, but this led to problems when coaches were found "dead" the next day, or the poles had not been reset from dewirements. Coaches were also parked in a lane different than the one assigned by the tower. The cost of lost time in the morning was greater than the cost of having operators park the cars as a team in the evening.

The group effort adds to an impersonal sense of goodwill at the day's end, making Potrero a great place to work. I am usually either exhausted or happy (or both) to see the car parkers and the revenue coworker who takes the money out of the fare box. I made it! Another day done, another dollar earned, still in one piece, and hopefully, without a trip upstairs to fill out paperwork. The best feeling is to get on my bike or walk to the bus stop and go home.

Pulling in and parking on the upper yard requires a skill level that takes time to master. There are switches in the yard and in the street, and if some are not working, it makes for a bad afternoon. There is rush hour traffic to contend with on 17th Street and a gauntlet to run through the tire shop garage. Coming to rest on the upper yard tracks is the challenge of navigating around parked cars that aren't supposed to be there. And the pressure of more buses coming home and backing up traffic on the street. Many thanks go to the traffic engineers who eliminated parking along 17th Street by our bus barn when 17th Street was recently repaved. This bike lane helps us get by in the morning and evening, and it helps the car parkers make their turn onto 17th!

Pulling out from the upper yard reminds me of the patience and Zen awareness I need with the equipment I am controlling, or it may control me.

# EPU

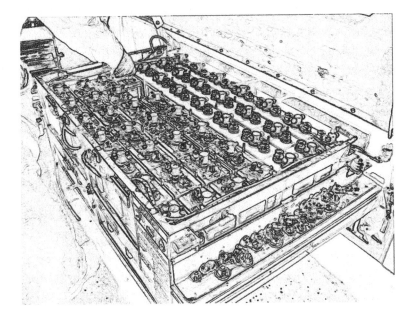

The switch to pull-out off of track five never works when we are late. Or, if once in a blue moon the yard starter's call to the overhead crew is answered, we have a working pull-out switch for three days. All the coaches behind the switch don't trigger the selectric box because the boxes are at an angle aligned for too sharp a right turn.

The same goes for Bryant outbound to 16th outbound and South Van Ness inbound to 16th outbound. But those two latter sets on the street are very rarely used, so it is of little import. The switch on track five is at a place where coaches pull out every day. We read the mantra from our superintendent that we are to pull out on time. A bulletin is put in our paddles as a reminder of our duties. We are also never to leave the coach once pre-op has started, but we're to call the OCC for assistance. The only problem is the Central Control Kingdom did not read our bulletin about calling for help with the problem switch. The Shop Kingdom did, and does beat to a drummer close to home. It is made aware of a bulletin we receive, and because of our many interactions throughout the day via the yard starter, we end up on a page very close to (or at least within) the same chapter of the same book. But getting the other kingdoms on the same page may never happen with Muni.

The Superintendent Kingdom is like a referee during a game. They are interested in rules violations similar to yellow flags, red flags, and penalty boxes. The only tools available are the rules. If the rules are not followed to the letter of the law, then a penalty results. These penalties are, in order, caution and reinstruct, warning, three-day suspension, five-day suspension, fifteen-day suspension, thirty-day suspension, and termination. If this progression of discipline is extended with a bold-faced warning an italicized warning, and a bold-faced, italicized warning, then I can relax somewhat. I have been given extra grace before suspension.

On the other side is Operator of the Month, System-wide Operator of the Year, and a monogrammed sweater and a check. The check is somewhere in the neighborhood of two-to-five hundred dollars. I can set this as a long-term goal before retirement, but I consider myself a success if I can learn from my mistakes, overcome adversity, and help others. This is the "Lojong" of finding Zen: overcoming adversity by meditation and practice. Increasing awareness of Eastern philosophy in our Western mindset is another aspect of this book. If there ever were adverse conditions to overcome, the life of a San Francisco transit operator provides the perfect opportunity for the Lojong. (See glossary.)

Getting back to the start of a day on track five. After the switch has been "fixed," I show the newer operators the trick to activate the switch by using the arrows painted on the lane as a guide to activating the electric correctly. Months go by before the overhead crew comes out again. I can hear them saying, "We just fixed it." Actually, I saw them working on the switch at the back of lane four the next day. If the message they received was to "fix the switch upon which we pull out," I can see how they would consider this other problem area, back by the wash rack, as an answer to this call.

As to the operator's point of view about getting things fixed, the wrong part or switch gets looked at due to confusion about where the problem is occurring. See the chapter, *The Overhead* for part descriptions and functions.

As a general rule, operators don't call Operations Central Control to report a faulty switch on track five. Instead of going on-air about a problem, we would remind the yard starter if we see her as we pass by the gate on epu. Epu is the battery power that the ETI coaches have so we can move without our poles on the wires. This epu pull-out is a good thing in that it forces us to check and see if our bus has battery power, should we need it later on in the day. We try to look for the good in every situation, as annoyance does nothing positive for our day, especially as we begin by pulling out on track five.

If in pre-op on a coach on five we find that our coach won't move in battery mode, we'll have a blocking situation whereby every coach behind this one will be late in pulling out. By following the instructions of bulletin PO 13-010, dated October 2, 2013, that we are not to leave our coach when pulling out, I call Central for assistance in my LPO. Central responds by asking me to locate the yard starter to meet the dead bus ahead blocking me. I respond by repeating the request, "Are you authorizing me to leave my coach to find the yard starter?" The terse reply begs the question that I can locate the yard starter faster than they can call.

But this has no foundation whatsoever in reality. Their job is to help us pull out on time. Period. But the institutional inertia is such that now their duties include a call they are not in the habit of making. Hence, you can see why we, as operators, remain silent in calling to fix the switch and to report another coach blocking and delaying our pull-out. Someone may end up in the penalty box.

We are also to cradle our poles in the harp before we move in epu mode. The yard is flat, and there is very little sway in the right turn we make, so in moist, foggy weather, we usually hit the poles' down button and move through from track five to four to the gate to put our poles back up. If we have good battery power, we cradle our poles and make the right turn out the gate and onto Bryant to return the poles to the wires. It is important to leave enough breathing room behind us for traffic to go around us safely as we put up our poles. This happened today as I pulled out, and all went well until crossing the first intersection at 17th and Bryant. My leader in the yard made a left turn on 17th to head for the 6 line. It was cold overnight, and we recently had lots of rain. The switches can be sticky until the sun has had its say. My poles followed his track to the left and I dewired. The selectric boxes did not reset the toggles after I passed by them straight on. Fortunately, my collectors did not catch on the wires, and I hit the poles' down button and checked to see if I was clear of any tangle. Good. I engaged epu to clear the intersection and to step to the back of the bus and cradle my poles in the harp.

When I got ready to put my poles back up, I noticed that I had no brasserie on the end of my pole. My collector ripped off the pole and was somewhere in the street. Okay, I'd better engage epu to the next safe location.

So here was a day when, before I even got into revenue service, I needed my epu three times, and I had only traveled two blocks! I was ordered by the inspector on the corner to pull the coach in on epu. Yes! I didn't have to wait for the shop. I knew I would have to fill out paperwork when I pulled in that evening, but I would make sure it was a good report. I took extra time to make my writing neat, clear, and easy to read. Many of us have the *can't-be-bothered* attitude when we want to hurry up and go home.

The unwritten rules are perhaps the most important to an operator in a trolley division. The unwritten rule of a short and concise report written with a good hand can go a long way to receiving a *cautionary* warning, and not a *warning*, especially not a **warning**, or hopefully not a **_warning!_** Keeping away from messy paperwork is keeping the Zen as a bus driver.

# THE LONG AND THE SHORT OF IT

After being called on the carpet for a pass-up on Van Ness, my leaving time from the North Point terminal was questioned by the assistant superintendent. I had departed about four minutes late. Thankfully, the data also showed I was four minutes late upon arrival. This information was obtained from using the sheets of data generated by our global positioning satellite. I had a short coach that day instead of the usual sixty foot articulated trolley. My response was that I had not been given the equipment I needed to perform my duties professionally.

I don't know exactly when it happened, but at some point, runs from Potrero were assigned a short coach for the 14 Mission lines and the 49 Van Ness buses. It is now acceptable practice to give certain runs a "short," forty foot coach instead of a sixty foot articulated trolley. I did a yard count of coaches a couple of years back, and out of one hundred fifty trolleys in the yard, only seventy-five were available. The other half had hold tags and needed parts for replacement. This changes everything about how to operate the line during the crunch zone. If you ever go by a bus barn during the day, notice how many trolleys are still in the yard. They are awaiting parts.

Running to an occupied bathroom, taking a stretch or getting a drink of water, make personal necessities seem like the cause of lost time in terms of recovery at the inbound terminal. The previous signup had given us twenty minutes at this time frame. This was cut to ten minutes, and as I would usually run four-to-six minutes late, I lost most of the time to recover. One operator walked off the job at this terminal and left the bus here at North Point because of the stress of the short recovery time at this inbound terminal.

So here I was in the assistant superintendent's office for disciplinary action because I ran out of room on my short coach after leaving the terminal late. In this case, a man using a cane had asked to be dropped off in the zone at Eddy farside, not nearside. I opened the door at a bus bulb where the sidewalk sticks out at the crosswalk. I did not know when he boarded, and couldn't see that he needed assistance due to a blocked view inside the crowded coach. He was sitting behind me in the "Black Hole," and he may have entered through the back door. Because the man was so calm in demeanor, his request so low in tone, I disregarded it and told him to exit nearside. My manager understands this use of the emergency rule, but I leave the hearing wondering about the outcome.

The use of GPS data is an excellent tool for obtaining leaving times of coaches, but it just gives a snapshot, not the big picture. When an inspector is present and observes the leaving times of several coaches over a period of at least thirty minutes, a realistic headway average is obtained, and traffic and driving conditions are much clearer. This is why I object to bringing up GPS data in a disciplinary hearing because "eyeball" physical presence is much more objective. I miss seeing the same inspector on the corner every day.

Inspectors are no longer stationed at checkpoints or relief points on a daily basis. Radio information about breakdowns, headway, and pull-in or pull-out orders are no longer available in-person on the street corner. As such, a rapport no longer develops between operators and the corner inspector. When I do call Central, I find that they think twenty minutes is too much time for a layover. This cutback, along with the lack of equipment, has made my senior driving years at Potrero a greater challenge in keeping the Zen.

On a recent Friday with a standard forty foot coach, I found that my leader in a sixty foot articulated trolley went out of service at the Ferry Terminal. I immediately adjusted to slow down and plan for a heavy trip. As I prepared to leave my last terminal, a man leaned on my coach and refused to move away from the side of the bus. On the previous Friday, a man pounded on my door to be let in while I was moving to the curb in battery mode, going around my leader who went on a 702 (radio code for personal necessity) break.

I now understand why these leaders go out of service around this time. The 14 line becomes the ninth level of hell during peak afternoon rush hour. Drinkers and emotionally distraught riders do not mix well with the downtown crowd just trying to go home from work. Heavy smokers and addicts with the aroma of coke or meth imbedded in their wool overcoats can be a triggering experience and make it hard to breathe. Trying to get the mix right of methadone and an 8-ball without an incident is an epic experience.

This is why calling for a 702, a twenty-minute break, may be required more often, especially from new hires because recovery time has been reduced. The long-term effects of less travel time may end up costing more by trying to in-fill employee absences with the daily detail. Hard to tell and hard to judge. I am grateful I learned the job when our division had over ninety daily hours of stand-by time. Now there are less than five hours of stand-by on the range sheet totals. (See the chapter on *Range Sheets* to understand all these other types of nondriving time.)

Pulling in on this particular holiday weekend Friday at my last stop at Ninth Street, a man refused to get up out of his seat, sitting in the Black Hole right behind the cockpit. My holiday weekend was being held up by an angry man who claimed I passed him up at a stop no one on board requested. Could I get him off the bus without incident, without damage to the front doors, or without causing a major medical emergency? Fortunately, he departed, but not without a rage-filled discourse. Whew! I called Central to clear a line delay, and my favorite operator wished me a good weekend. *Yes!* A friend at Central Control!

But the agony of the mental twist is about paperwork on a holiday weekend pull-in. To me, this is why a job as a civil service worker on the line with the public, is the reason many of my friends stay away from putting in a job application—because of *the people*. This reading may not capture your imagination, but believe me, when you are sitting behind the wheel, it is a big deal.

Now, how could I write this up without going to a pass-up hearing at 1 South Van Ness? I keep hearing the angry, bloody man calling in my cap and coach number as he sat behind me on his cell phone while I prepared to pull in at Tenth. Was he really making the call or just trying to mess with me emotionally? As he chided me for negligence and being inconsiderate, I couldn't help but break out in a Cheshire grin. My biggest fear, getting another pass-up PSR, was unfolding before my very eyes.

If I mentioned a bloody face, my failure to ask for medical assistance could show a lack of empathy. But was it also reasonable to assume that I was protecting those on board from a medical emergency by not allowing him on the bus? I had passed by the bus shelter before I saw him madly waving at me, and it seemed a toss-up as to whether the pass-up was valid or not. I had another woman complain that I did not pick her up here, although I had stopped and opened my doors a few weeks earlier. Ironically, there she was, sitting in the bus shelter, looking at her smart phone for the next limited stop rapid coach as the bloody man came running. I had scored a victory about reading head sign destination with her complaint, but here was another.

This is the dilemma we face in a split second choice to pass up or pick up. But it is hard to intuit all of this in the seconds of passing by the bus shelter. The trend lately has been to make the stop and let it play. So, I considered this to be an error on my part. How much of a big deal it could depend on how honest I was. This job provides the ultimate opportunities for patience and adventure.

It's now been two weeks since several angry passenger incidents (including those above), and all is calm. I have had nothing but smiles and thanks. It seems lunar or astrological in the timing. My personality remains the same, the equipment is still a short coach, yet all is well. I question my blame on the equipment. Now it seems not so genuine.

When an old, long coach dogs you on the doors, it can be like a slow motion train wreck where the buses pile up behind you as you drag down the line. After some meditation and prayer that I be shown what to do, I did have to admit that the coaches I had been given were defect-free. The short coaches moved and caused no mechanical delay. My frustration had been at the back door jam-up, not with the performance of the vehicle.

I had one of those great, *Electra Glide in Blue* days, with no one in front of me or behind me. Central Control informed me I did not have a leader, and I could move up four. Yes!. No write-up at 30th for being hot. No one dragging me down in an old, long coach. Freedom. I was shown the grace of having a small coach and why my desire for a long coach was misplaced. Go tell it to the mountain. I eventually got two unpaid days off for too many pass-up complaints. Oh well, suck it up and continue to march. We learn early on that tomorrow is another day.

This is truly the long and short of it when it comes to keeping Zen (and my job) as a trolley man. New prototypes are being built now for delivery and will hopefully be ready for revenue service towards the latter part of 2015. This new equipment, sixty brand-new articulated trolleys from Canada, via Seattle, will change the nature of our job. Clean, functioning equipment that actually moves faster down the road is like building extra minutes onto our paddle; it also lessens physical stress in our knees and legs because braking and acceleration are new and responsive.

We may get several lost lines back with this new equipment because we did not have enough long coaches. Heard tell that a nearby bus barn will house the short trolleys, and our barn may be housing long coaches only. It makes sense, as sixty new long coaches will take up much more track space than what we have now. If I can just hold on long enough and keep the Zen!

# BIG MOUTHS AND CRY-BABIES

"Big mouths run hot." So says our elected leader in the receiver's office before picking up my outfit one morning. Apparently, a common thread running through arguments rebutting a write-up for running ahead of schedule is that of complaining about other persons, places, or things like our equipment as causes for running ahead of schedule. But it doesn't take much to understand the simplicity of why a bus is ahead of schedule; it's the operator behind the wheel.

And I have found myself in big-mouth mode often. In fact, before a suspension hearing, my union rep repeated to me (as he does every time I am in trouble), "You talk too much," or "You ask too many questions." And he is right. I find myself asking how I got into this mess, and in retrospect, it becomes clear that I just need to shut-up or say that I don't know. Others are trying to help me by giving hints or obvious clues to tip off silence, but my monkey-Gemini mind seems incapable of holding back.

And holding back is a valid technique to avoid running hot. Running hot is running ahead of schedule by more than one minute. Most of my friends and riders give a look of disbelief when they hear that we are not allowed to run one minute ahead of schedule. With on-time performance so low, I understand why this rule may seem over the top, and I agree. But, like my manager says, the first step to run on time is to leave on time and not to run ahead of schedule. There seems to be less of a concern from management in running late, but as someone in the seat out on the road, running late has many consequences, none of which is as uncomfortable as the seat in the superintendent's office.

Running late in the Mission between 18th and 23rd almost always results in no terminal time at the end of the line. Use of the kneeler for walkers and use of the lift for laundry carts and wheelchairs can drag down other trolleys. Loss of terminal time may not necessarily take any emotional toll or add to stress. So, although the bus is very crowded in this middle-of-the-line crunch zone, the consequence of complaint or accident is low. Outbound from the Ferry, however, I have found that getting too crowded *does* influence complaints and service disputes. So it is *where we are running late* that influences our trip. Getting into the crunch early on is bad news. The chance of going out of service goes way up.

As passengers, you would do well to look and see if another bus is coming. Use the clock inside the shelter to see if one is following in a few minutes. It is the use of this kind of resource that can make our railway run more smoothly. Please stop and take a look at this aspect of passenger load on the operator and the drama that ensues when no more seats or aisle space is available. Whether it is an operator crying at the barn or a passenger screaming in the aisle, use the next bus clock to your advantage. Good things come to those who wait.

# WE'VE BEEN WAITING AN HOUR

"Where the hell have *you* been?"

a) "The pizza delivery boy was late and apologized, so I got a free pizza and ate it all at the terminal. You don't expect me to wolf it all down in five minutes, do you? I am not allowed to use my phone while I am driving, so I had to call my order in after I got to the end."

b) "The brakes failed, and I had to wait for the shop after filling out an accident report for the three beamers I took out rolling down Russian Hill. The shop wanted me to fill the bus up with as many people as possible to see if the brakes would hold."

c) "I did some shopping at Fisherman's Wharf and don't want you to rain on my parade. Wait here for the next bus right behind me so I can pick up the folks at the next stop. Since you've waited an hour already, another fifteen minutes is nothing."

d) "I'm terribly sorry for this delay. I am in a hurry with a triple load and don't have time to argue with you. You can get on the next bus right behind me." Shut the door and drive off.

The correct answer is, of course, b). This gains sympathy from the angry mob and gives an accurate view of the equipment and service. Also, it hints that affluent owners of hi-end vehicles will get their due. This unites the angry mob in a can-do attitude.

Although this may not be an actual verbatim test question provided during the civil service exam, the insight provided here may improve your skill score. As a transit professional, you are required to handle difficult situations quickly and respond to questions without hesitation. While some books on the subject of driving a bus may provide guidance as to how to remain calm in a dense, congested city such as San Francisco, let's face it, we may not have the patience or time to assume a lotus position and meditate.

When intending passengers become a large mob, it doesn't bode well for my day. If BART is shut down or our metro tunnel is blocked, large numbers of commuters congregate at our trolley and motor coach surface stops. I need the space in my head to answer questions, and still pull away in a timely fashion. I also have to maintain space at the front of the aisle so I can see out my mirrors and the front door.

I took a cab home the other day, and the cabbie said that on a talk radio show, a regular caller was complaining that our buses run around empty and that funding should be cut. I laughed and said that the reason our buses are empty is because they are being towed back to the shop. Our trolleys are up to twenty years old and "go to sleep," especially in hot weather.

This caller obviously was a car person who may never have taken mass transit. I can assure the readers that our buses are crowded from morning rush well into the night at 10:00 p.m. Our 22 and 14 lines never really run empty. A safety officer imported from another city commented how amazing he thought it was that our buses were still crowded hours after rush hour. So, seriously then, we need new trolleys, and we need them now!

If I try to use this reasoning with the riding public paying their "fare" share, they usually become angry. They say I am going to make my money regardless of what they do or do not put in the fare box, and they are correct. I just believe it adds to a lawless kind of attitude that doesn't take personal responsibility. Those who are grateful for our transit system pay their fare and are generally courteous and helpful. Keeping Zen means keeping my side of the street clean and not worrying about what others do.

# STOP REQUEST

One defect that does not usually appear on the defect card is that of a stop request. Most of the time as operators, we become so familiar with our routine that we almost don't need the stop request lights or bell to know where and when people are getting off the bus. Likewise, we know where we must stop and open the doors, even if it first appears that no one is intending to board in the zone. Hospital stops are a no-brainer for stopping and lowering the kneeler automatically. Certain stops around corners and with limited sight distance are also good places to stop, even if we hear no ring. Hermann is such a stop on the 22, as is Kansas, before turning towards 17th. Recent changes to our operating rules made by voter initiatives and technology have given a strong voice to our riding public and have provided managers with tools to enforce the rules and make those of us who operate the buses more accountable for our actions.

It used to be that you guys were just as tired and fed up (as we were) when you were on your ride home, so there was no way you were going to dial the Muni number on your land line to an office that was by then closed about being passed up by a Muni bus.

Today, with cell phone in hand and a simple 3-1-1 on speed dial, a call can be placed immediately and a written record and ID number generated on the spot. When I was being observed, I received a call within five minutes from Central Control about someone I had passed up three stops back. Wow! That is a big change from the first ten years I spent behind the wheel with only the land line number, 673-M.u.n.i. So even if I put in a miscellaneous form, no way was I getting out of a hearing or discipline on pass-ups on the 49.

The bottom line I learned from all this was that not observing the one block spacing rule can get me in trouble when my leader is close in front, and another bus (such as the 14) is behind me. I have to realize that new riders are not hip on how to signal a coach at a multiple-line stop. Not being *ready* is not a valid excuse as a pass-up. The only one needed to be taught a lesson was me!

Twelfth and Otis is one of those "around the corner" stops that need be made, even if we don't see anybody waiting as we turn the corner on the 49 from S. Van Ness to Otis Street. A coworker recently commented on a PSR he got for a pass-up at this stop. No one was waiting at the stop and he kept on going. I, too, have done this many times but have been written-up for accumulating too many of these no-stop bus stop actions. Coaches send digital information from their onboard mother board about how many times we open the doors, for how long, and at what stop. Every action on the bus is recorded, including PA-announced stops.

With the simplicity of calling a three-digit number (311) and a digital camera file in cloud storage (not on a 72 hour loop that erases and re-records), those of us who have been around for ten- plus years must adapt to this change. We must realize that pass-ups to manage our passenger load or headway must be made—even if they cause intending passengers a delay in boarding a coach. Coming to the curb and opening the door may no longer be enough to satisfy the requirement for making a stop. Moving away from the curb can only be done if there is no bill-boarding (restricted view, such as the inability to see around) from other large vehicles. Hence a four second spacing rule between such large vehicles, to keep the view ahead maximized.

It's difficult to override a habit I have developed over a period of time. I have been so obsessed with continuing to make the schedule at all costs that I have reduced dwell time in the zone at certain stops. I am overcoming this tendency by trying to stay in one place and keep my doors open longer. Still, there are some late-runners that don't make it in time, and I have to let go of the outcome. I must be clear of fear as to whether latecomers will call in on 3-1-1 and complain that I passed them up. There appears to be an invisible ledger of karma that can keep trouble at bay if I have waited for runners. The same is true for right-of-way with other cars. God usually gives me a signal that my grace is about ready to expire. If close calls start occurring with unusual frequency, I immediately pray for a larger space cushion between vehicles and waiting for passengers to board and sit.

There seems to be an increased perception from those who miss my bus that I am not doing my job when I do not stop. I accumulate too many pass-up notices within a three-month time frame. Once again, our mirrors only capture a small zone alongside our bus, and we may not see someone running from across the street or perpendicular to where our coach is standing. Just yesterday, as a passenger, I saw this happen several times while occupying the last seat at the back of the bus. People would run from the BART station steps on the side of the bus, and *I* could see them running, but the operator could not see them and pulled away. This makes us look bad, but we aren't intentionally passing them up.

This hasn't been easy, especially with new riders. I have to do what has been suggested: slow down and not worry about a full bus. These are the two biggest demons I have had to fight on the job with headway changes, and if I can cross the retirement ribbon finish line with my operator status in good standing, I will have crossed victorious! Keeping Zen is all the challenge I will ever need. And it is as basic as this topic and the action in a stop request.

# LATE RING

I approach a stop that I sometimes pass up without a ring or without anyone standing on the curb. Still no chime or no dash light. I coast without accelerating. I make the decision to stay in the traffic lane and pass the point of pulling to the right to bring the door to the curb. I pass the bus stop. "Wait, wait! I pulled the cord!" Most times, I can flag stop the coach and let them off. But at other times, I must continue forward to the next safe space. This does not always go over well. Anger arises because I pass by a stop. And I have come to use my intuition to know when this is likely to happen. Sure enough, I can stop without a ring at a baby stop and see someone exit the back door without a ring. Indeed, operators with years of experience do develop extra sensory perception.

And after trial and error of being told about our mother or our birthright, we adapt our sixth sense as to when and where we will need to stop without a request. Greenwich on Van Ness, Kansas or Hermann on the 22 line, and 29th Street on the 49. The list goes on.

There are glitches within the DVAS and GPS which cause just enough of a delay in ringing a stop that I have learned where these are, have slowed accordingly and have called out a stop just to make sure. Even then, I still must find the closest safe place to come to rest and let someone out. I have learned it is easier to just let them off as soon as possible rather than go to the next stop. As a line trainer, I let my student know where these places and stops are, so they don't have to go through a painful learning curve. As with many things, the devil is in the details.

When the doors close, and the bus begins moving, this is an okay time for a passenger to pull the chord for the next stop. Or at least a block and a half away from the next zone. If we are making a turn, you have to understand that our eyes are focusing on pedestrian threats and traffic, not on the overhead stop request display. If no chime sounds, please be aware of this. Most conflict arises from the assumption that the chime sounded when it did not. As operators, we note where this happens frequently, and stop and open the door automatically. If we don't, then sure enough, the battle cry comes forth from the back door. This is how you, the passengers, can train us, the bus drivers.

We, too, can train you to ring at the correct moment; otherwise, you get dinged by having to walk back to the previous stop. Ringing late for Broadway and Steiner means you are going to Vallejo. To those reading these words on a flat sheet (such as a map), you may not realize the hill involved between these two stops. If, for example, you want Nob Hill on the 1 Line inbound, and you don't get off at Taylor, you are in for a rude awakening for the Fairmont on Mason. The uphill grade is the maximum allowed before a street becomes a staircase!

Truck drivers unfamiliar with the streets of San Francisco find out about our grade changes the hard way, as do tour bus drivers. A large tow truck must be employed to get the vehicle clear from a cross street scrapping whereby the long, seven-ton vehicle or trailer must be removed from the wedge created by a flat street crossing on a steep grade. I hope the Union 76 Truck Stop outside of Sacramento has a grade map near the break room for drivers heading into town from the Midwest.

New riders can always be found out by the way they depart. They are the culprits of the late ring or of no ring at all. "I rang the bell!" Sitting on the back bench, they wait until the bus has come to a complete stop before they get up from their seat. They try to make their way through the aisle to the back door. By then, the regulars have stepped down to activate the doors and are long gone. As the doors begin to shut, they step down after the doors close, and I am ready to leave the zone. I know where these late-bloomers lie, so I have learned to look at the back door one last time to see if some person or group is holding us up.

Sure enough, the "late-ring-crowd" finally makes it down the steps. When I am training a new operator, my extra set of eyes can help the student be alert to when and where this happens. It always comes at the worst times—when we are late and without a leader. Often, we get behind the wheel to move up our coach into a better headway. God, please help this book find itself into the hands of a late ringer. Keep the Zen!

# MOTOR COACH

When our barn falls short of equipment, we are assigned to Woods Division to get a diesel or motor coach. I love trolleys, and I love that San Francisco did not do away with streetcars and trolleys. Nowadays, trolleys look like buses. They have rubber tires and the body of a bus, except for the fact that they have two poles on the roof that attach to double wires carrying 600 volts of direct current. Because our tires are rubber, we need to have a second ground wire to complete the circuit. Though I have designated this book's title as from a bus driver's perspective, I am actually driving a trolley. My range of motion and ability to change lanes is more restricted because I trolley my poles on the overhead wires. Operators of trolleys must always be aware of the dead points or breakers in the overhead and never exceed their operating range. They should always keep in mind the range and length of the poles on the roof of the bus.

Historically, streetcars look much like the barn style trolley and have only one pole in their roof because the steel wheels on the rails are grounded by the earth. Streetcars came into casual conversation as they became more streamlined in the 1950s during the PCC era. The term "trolley," when spoken, came to mean the cable car style of body that was square-like and made of wood. The cow-catcher or people-catcher in front of the cab was a good thing to have along Market Street. The density of people boarding on multiple tracks is a wonder to behold in the historic photos of the time. I find it interesting that these days we have concrete islands between lanes on Market Street to keep boarding safe, now that the trolleys no longer have people-catchers. But there are times along Mission Street that I wish we still had them.

Most of my coworkers are not too thrilled to have to go to an alien division and operate a motor coach in place of a trolley when our barn simply does not have a coach available for us. I do, however, like the motor coaches for the 22 Fillmore line, because the back doors are wider and further to the rear. This feature helps with the aisle crowding and speeds boarding and alighting. I also like the fact that the middle door step is not the abracadabra mechanism on a motor coach. I can click the rear doors shut, even if people are standing on the back steps. When heavy and late, the motor coach can be a life-saver for my emotional state.

Anyway, I am down with motor coaches and don't mind going over to Woods to pick up one. I actually like the ride over on my bike. The Dogpatch behind Potrero Hill is actually an interesting neighborhood that seems like it is in the country, miles from the city. And yet the skyline is right there in front of you when you look down from the hill. This is where much filming takes place because of the dramatic, unobstructed view of skyline. The movie *Bullet* was shot on Pennsylvania Avenue just up from Dogpatch on Potrero Hill. When I say up, do I mean up! The escarpment here, from the ramp and the bay to the vistas of downtown, is dramatic, as is the over-crossing on 280 Freeway on the 22 line. We climb from Dogpatch to Potrero Hill. This is definitely a place to keep the Zen!

# OPEN TRENCH

The San Francisco Water Department and Pacific Gas and Electric are constantly opening up the street to repair and maintain the city's infrastructure. Repaving the street is usually scheduled after many such repairs are made, so just because it looks like construction is finished, there may still be more lane closures coming. When all the trenches are finished, it is a good sign that a nice, smooth street surface is just around the corner. I love seeing the big asphalt ripper chewing up the asphalt after several weeks of open trenches because it means fewer dewirements when the new surface is finished and less rattling in the cage. I can hear myself think and answer a question you may have because there is less shaking going on over potholes and rough seams. Those metal plates can cause rough operation if we can't go around them.

Many times the construction guys are unfamiliar with how much operating room we need to pass a lane closure. If the cones are set down between the hash marks separating the closed lane, we can make it through. But we cannot pass by an area with one-and-a-half lanes closed off if there is a nearby turn, or the wires are slightly to the right of center of the closed-off lane. The details of the permit become imperative. Because at the railway, we need to know if we will have to make a battery-powered pass of a lane closure or open trench. Timing is also a key factor regarding peak period and traffic conditions. What may be okay during lunch may be a long delay during rush hour. Or because traffic density can be hard to guess, what should be no big deal can create an awful bottleneck if just one trolley gets blocked or dewires too far from the power lines and has no battery power.

I learned early on that if I saw any construction bulletins in my paddle when I pull out in the morning, I had better check to see if my coach has epu or apu auxiliary power. If battery fluids are checked regularly, then a coach has strong battery power. But if the batteries run dry, the energy storage becomes weak, and entire sets of batteries need to be reordered. This can get expensive. Our trolleys contain racks of batteries. So, looking at the battery gauges during pre-op is always a good idea. If you don't, finding out about battery storage in the middle of a construction zone right off of a freeway exit ramp can really tie things up.

Even though operators seem to get blamed for a lot of problems, it is amazing how just a quick check of power or a look at a gauge can make a big difference down the road. Keeping Zen means knowing whether or not the coach has enough power to cross construction on battery power alone.

# BUTTONHOOK

Four foot right side clearance is a must at all times when driving a bus, especially for a right turn. Double-parked vehicles, pedestrians standing off the curb, and cyclists standing on their cranks past the stop line are all hazards that make the buttonhook right turn necessary. A buttonhook turn is one in which we make a wide sweep to the left before making a right turn so our wheels have enough clearance as we finish the turn.

The first question a motorist or pedestrian would do well to understand is, *Am I blocking transit by stopping here?* By using the mirrors and scanning every five-to-eight seconds, it soon becomes clear what distinguishes a professional driver from an unskilled motorist. Likewise, cyclists who are new to riding a bike in the city become apparent at a red light or bus zone.

When a new curb clear is installed on a corner, and a new ramp is cut at the crosswalk, I make the call to Central to create a record about a corner that has not yet been painted red. A curb clear is that red zone on a trolley turn needed to complete a turn without crossing into the oncoming lane. Motorists begin parking on a curb clear that is not marked in red, and this creates problems for clearance in turning.

Many of my friends seem dubious about driving such a large vehicle in a city, but when turns are made wide enough and set up before the corner, things are much easier. I feel more comfortable driving a bus than a car in the city because I have more mirrors. My mirrors are bigger, my vehicle is larger, and it has more lights.

What gets me is when cars double park or when they are left unattended on a curb clear where we need the space to make a turn without dewiring.

Getting the red paint on a new curb clear may not stop a vehicle from parking there, but it does make most people move when we come from behind. Anything I can do to improve the odds of having a clear turn helps me to keep the Zen.

# JAY WALKERS

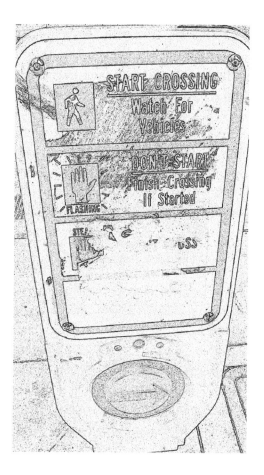

Back East, I remember seeing the "no jaywalking" signs on the poles on almost every arterial in NYC and Philly. But here in San Fran, we are a part of the wild, wild, West where "Every which way but loose" (to coin a phrase from a favorite Eastwood flick) applies. As any passenger and driver can attest, pedestrians here are among the most *entitled* of any city in the world. This fact can lead to daredevil, death-defying acts in traffic and at intersections. It's almost as though the new countdown crosswalk clocks are a stopwatch and starting gun to begin the race to the other side. For others, the line drawn in the sand—the crosswalk—is about as important as attempting to mark the high tide mark on a beach where the waves have left their foam outline.

The flashing stop hand does not mean *wait at the corner.* Your time has passed. It actually means *run like hell,* especially if I keep my front door open at the corner. Or, if jaywalking casually across Van Ness, the stop lights and crosswalk signals mean absolutely nothing. And the dance is simply to pause between vehicles rushing by. Perhaps they will stop, perhaps they will honk, or perhaps you will finger them or hit them hard with your fist.

We are all constantly teaching each other a lesson about consequence. This is particularly true if we have been up partying all weekend followed by the famous "morning after" walk of shame. As a bus driver, I see it all. The dark, bug-eyed sunglasses on a gray morning. The twitch of the jaw. The evasive look away. Or the loud cry of anger, complete with descriptive, profane poetry.

All that matters as a trolley man intent on getting the next paycheck is to check left-right-left on my thirteen mirrors, all hopefully pointed to one space above my shoulders in the driver's seat. I may have to do a "Sugar Ray" and bounce my head back and forth a bit if the rocker arms on the side of the bus have been frozen out of alignment by the wash rack at the barn. All-in-all, the moments after closing the doors are as important as becoming the next blog on social internet or front page news in the paper. All I ask is that you make some noise if you are crossing from behind my mirrors in my blind spot. Please and thank you!

# BIKE RACK V. THE WIGGLE

Most bike riders are fast to load their bike on the bike rack that drops down over the front bumper. They tag-in and are gone to the back of the coach. I can guess where they are going to get off, but it is a good idea to let operators know where they plan to take the bike off of the rack. Many a day when I pull in, I find bikes waiting in the Lost and Found area. These are bikes left on the rack when the bus pulls in. Most cyclists don't communicate with the operator when they board. It is not a requirement that we know where the bike is coming off, but it is a good idea, especially if the drop-off is a long way from the where the bike gets put on the rack.

On a warm day, cyclists waiting to board a crosstown run on the 33 Ashbury on 18th Street usually can't put their bike on the rack because it is full. If they wait by Mission, they can get a place on the rack. But by Delores Park, it is too late to get on. The bike rack takes two bikes only, so when a third rider is intending, I let him/her take the bike (if it is a light racer or a ten-speed) up the back steps to the rear aisle where there is a large gap in the seats. Most of the time, when a cyclist sees the rack is full they sigh or shrug and get on their bike to ride around the hill.

We have a bypass that goes crosstown for cyclists called "The Wiggle." This is a bike path that follows streets around the Haight-Ashbury hill. A person new to town does not understand that it is possible to get from the Mission to the Haight without going up any major hill. In San Francisco, we have forty three hills over forty nine square miles. This means we have one hill for every 1.1 square miles. Although the city is not one continuous grid pattern, most hills can be avoided by simply jogging over one block.

This is why San Francisco is a much more bike-friendly city than Seattle or San Diego. There is no way to avoid Capitol Hill if trying to ride from Pike Place Market to Lake Washington. It is possible to get to Ballard and Fremont from downtown without a hill via Myrtle-Edwards or Eastlake, but there is quite a long distance around Queen Anne hill to get there.

So even though Seattle is built on seven hills like Rome and has seven times fewer hills than San Francisco, the escarpment of the Denny regrade and of Queen Anne or Magnolia makes for intense climbs on narrow streets that really are not safe for bikes. True, I love the fact that you can park a car in either direction on either side of a residential street, but trying to ride down a street with an opposing car makes for intense awareness at corners. Hence, the imperative red zones by the stops signs at corners. I see why Seattle is so meticulous about painting its curb clears; there is no other space for a vehicle to wait for an oncoming car. And adding a bike to the mix seems next to scary. Thank God for the Burke-Gilman bike path. Rainier Valley has steep side streets on the south side, and the Renton highlands act like a barrier to South Center or Longacres.

San Diego's mesas and valleys are so long and unforgiving one would have to be in professional racing fitness to keep going. The Fashion Valley shopping area makes the climb to Hillcrest look like a training course for running a marathon or grand prix race in France. To get from Mission Beach to anywhere else but downtown seems like an uphill battle. Even Banker's Hill and the long upgrade by Balboa Park to Hillcrest seem to make for an unfriendly bike city. Plus, motorists are probably not used to seeing cyclists in traffic. I can understand riding a bike in and around Hillcrest for short errands, but I did not see too many cyclists in San Diego or in transit on the buses.

Portland has a bike culture, and I will have to try riding there some time. I hear the trail near the river to the south is nice, and the gradual upgrade on the Hawthorne side does seem gentle enough. The number of bridges they have seems to make the crossing to downtown not that bad.

But boy, can I see flying down the grade inbound like a zoo bomber for some close calls! Portland does appear to resemble San Francisco in being the most accommodating city for cyclists on the West Coast. And with the transit centers placed around the city, transfers seem to be reliable. I can always tell I have a visitor from Portland when they ask me where the nearest transit center is located.

So let me know when you're getting off. This comment goes unacknowledged by most bike riders as they walk back down the aisle with their helmet still on. Rare is the day that a cyclist actually stops to talk to the bus driver. Hence, the collection of bikes I find by the dispatcher as lost and found when I pull in at night. I can also tell when the bus driver is not attentive to the needs of a cyclist. Noting a bus moving around town with the bike rack empty but still down like a people-catcher is not safe.

# FRISCO

When an OG (old gangster) or ex-Muni driver enters the coach, puffed up with stories of experience and history, it is always better to let them run their course without interruption. The easy part is they don't give you a chance to speak anyway. Heaven help a big mouth (such as me) should I try to interrupt or question a point made from someone who has lived in "Frisco." The biggest challenge to a problem passenger are ex-Muni drivers who no longer work for the railway and not necessarily because they made it to regular retirement. Those who have been drivers can be the worst problem-child onboard because they know the rules, and they know what can strike an emotional imbalance with an operator.

I love it when they test me and find no one home, which is to say, I don't take the bait, or no fish are biting today. When they smile as they depart, they know I know, and that I have withstood the test of time to make it past rookie stage. In a way, this is an unwritten medal of honor that shows them I know what it takes to not have an attitude and get them to the curb without drama. I think I like this about driving in Frisco, more than stopping at the Transbay Terminal or train station.

# RETRIEVERS

These are the two bulbs that sit on the back of the trolley below the back window. In the ETI coaches, the spools are hidden in the back compartment below the rear window. Some coaches have a lever to reset them; others can be reset by pulling on the rope and de-spooling some slack. The retrievers all have different tensions and different points of reset and click. During pre-op, I find it a good idea to tug on the ropes to see how much tension a spool has and how sensitively it would retrieve the rope and bring down the pole should the retriever spring be activated. If a spool is slightly bent, it can cut the rope quick and abruptly.

Many a shoulder or back injury has resulted in not knowing the strength or tension on the rope from the retriever. I have been blessed by not getting caught with a bad one. Always better to follow the rules and place one rope at a time back on the wires, especially when the collectors don't want to pivot to follow the wire. I have learned to never stand under the wire when I put my pole back up, particularly when wet. The nasty black stain of carbon that drops on my hat or uniform may never come out. It can be a long time before a new uniform part can be ordered.

# ROAD CALL

"Road Call, Road Crew." This announcement can be heard in the Potrero Yard when two members of the shop are required to do a service call on a bus that breaks down on the street during revenue service. This pit stop is a good way to make sure the bus I am passing on to the next operator will not have the same problem later. I like to think that I have good karma with the bus I am to receive from a coworker, based upon my care in passing along a bus that has been fixed by a road call. And by being meticulous with the defect card and honest with the shop, I get the answers I need about stuff that goes wrong.

I recently had to pull in a low-power coach, and the tower needed to know what was specifically wrong with the power. I gave them the code numbers I saw the road crew came out to clear, and this detail helped save guesswork about what was wrong with the coach. If someone pulls a coach in without being clear about the problem, I can understand why it doesn't get fixed. Calling out the road crew has been helpful in making sure I know what to tell the tower when I bring the coach into the barn. I complain less about a defect with a coach knowing I have become reliable in filling out the defect card and being specific about the problem. The perception of doing my part gets me a clear picture of why something is not getting fixed when I gain a certain level of trust with the road crew, the shop in general, and when I pull into the tower after a long day.

Some problems are solved with such a simple action, that I try to learn what I can do to make a problem go away and stay in service.

## Front door won't close

I check to see if the wheelchair lift has shifted over time by traveling over rough pavement and turns with dips. Activating the lift and stowing it speeds up the front door close. If air is not getting to the doors, I can play with the butterfly valve to see if a more solid position enhances the channel of air to the doors. Sometimes, the kneeler is not all the way up from past use. Clicking the up button helps.

## No forward traction on power pedal

Shut the coach down and reset master control. If a foot touches both the service brake and the power pedal, the traction sensor will shut down. Awareness of this simple safety feature and simply rebooting the coach, can save hours of down time and missing headway. On certain coaches, one must wait a full two minutes to restart the bus; otherwise, the computer gets confused, and the bus will not budge until the shop comes to reset the warnings.

## Lift will not store

I see the warning light come on when the lift is in use. The motor stalls, and I can hear my bus groaning and complaining about the extra accessory use on the batteries. I immediately shut down the blowers or any other accessory when using the lift. Moving to up or down while on stow or changing the direction of the polarity gets the lift moving again. Sometimes stamping down on the lift flap under the middle step prevents the block from stowing the lift. On an older model, getting out and pushing the lift in gets us on our way. This is a two-man job, so help from the passengers is necessary.

# Kneeler will not rise

When the air is low or the coach is loaded, best not to use the kneeler. I have had to override my natural tendency to keep moving and to wait for the kneeler to rise. This prevents a flat tire, which is when the tire becomes damaged from scraping on the wheel well because the air in the suspension system has not fully recovered.

# Rear doors won't close

If I control when the rear doors open and close, I have seen this problem go away. By letting the doors close passively after a person steps on the middle treadle step, the doors hang. The position of the ER door opener is in an unfavorable dash location, so we must lean forward to operate this toggle. Bad ergonomic design is the number-one problem with the rear door controller of our imported trolleys. The last of the buses designed by operators, to my knowledge, were the MCIs by Greyhound. Operator input to engineers or desktop designers to determine where to place the door opener is critical—not just window dressing.

# Wiper stops moving

Get out and push! Coaxing the wiper can get it going if the motor is on from the inside, and the wiper won't budge. The biggest factor in creating this problem is leaving the wipers on at a terminal after it stops raining. After a while, the hypnotic back and forth metronome effect of the arms makes them become invisible to our awareness, especially if the light patter of rain stops ever so gradually as we enter our terminal. The blades can smudge and scar the windscreen so that visibility suffers on the next bright day. Leaving the wipers on dulls the blade and results in a complete smearing of the window when they are turned back on in the next rain storm. Only after several minutes of use does the wiper keep the view clean, and even then, it's with a hope and a prayer.

## Body fluids on the seats

It's sometimes a challenge to identify what that is on the seat by trying to remember who sat where. This is when setting interior rear mirrors makes a difference. Seriously, this is a big deal, and it looks like God is trying to tell me something about my conduct with respect to fluids and trash left on the bus. I don't call for the car cleaners, as I believe my best choice is to stay in service and not create a gap between buses. This rock-hard responsibility from Saturn, coupled with Mercury retrograde in communication with my boss or my union of coworkers, can set off an unbalance in the scales not unlike a thermonuclear testing of a bomb. Who dropped the bomb? I did.

I have to take the road less traveled, which is usually the high road, to keep my integrity on tap. Otherwise, I am spinning out of control and in danger of colliding with my coworkers and destroying the peace and rhythm of the line. Am I putting someone down or some job on the line by taking care of business myself? I can't seem to get Central Control on my side with a pull-in conducive to the least disruption of service by pulling in outbound by the barn at Bryant and getting a new coach, rather than taking a coach out of service at the inbound terminal. I have to surrender this, mind my own business, and not judge others by what I think they should do. And trying to find the time and place for stating my piece is a challenge. But never fear, for a conference with the superintendent is imminent if I go too far too fast.

The best offense is a good defense. If I can prevent an unsanitary condition from arising on the bus, I need to do this at the door before boarding, not at a terminal during peak period.

# THE OVERHEAD

The differences our corridor streets have that most cities have lost are the sets of wires over the center of the lanes. We have numerous utility poles alongside the sidewalk with support wires holding the power. These traveling wires conduct electric power from our hydroelectric grid. Our O'Shaunessy Dam is one valley north of the Yosemite Valley and provides not only drinking water, but power for our trolleys. I love the fact that our city uses this carbon-free source of power for our extensive trolley lines. We have more miles of trolley wire than any other city in the world. I am proud to work for a railway that has so many different modes of equipment. I can call myself a bus driver, but not use any fossil fuels when picking up passengers. I feel as an active agent helping our Earth stay as clean as possible.

Our overhead requires routine maintenance, and it is common to see our big yellow trucks working on the wires over the street. Now, all of our trolleys are equipped with battery power or APU, auxiliary power unit, to go around a crew working on the wires overhead. There are sets of trays of batteries that power this mode. This is another technology change that makes life much easier than in the day when we had to roll around an obstacle or get pushed by another trolley. Gone are the days when passengers would be asked to step outside and help push the bus through an intersection or dead area at a breaker crossing. Before bicycle racks were mounted on the front bumper, we could push a dead-in-the-water trolley from behind with another trolley.

I try to learn about the parts and pieces of the overhead whenever I see the crew taking a break, or just having finished doing a repair. I like to know their terms for things, so if I have to call in a repair, I can at least give Central Control an idea about what I am talking about.

The biggest reason nothing gets done is that the wrong switch or converge is being described on the radio. It is difficult to call in a specific problem in detail when in a driving mode—an alert, problem-solving state of mind. This is a different part of the brain than the one that answers a question about the number of stops away from a destination or a part location while in a complex intersection of lots of special work (many switches and crossovers). Without knowing the standard name for a part, any damage report is left open to misunderstanding about where the maintenance is needed. Try as I might, I haven't been able to convince those outside of training to add this information to our syllabus. Line trainers become the key.

## Crossovers

If you ever look up in the middle of an intersection where two trolley lines meet, you will see crossovers. Below these are the fiberglass slots along the traveling wires and jump-over wire bridging the gap, so to speak, over the dead area where the wires cross. This setup insulates the positive and negative wires from touching one another. We must power off our coach as we coast through this dead area. That is what those yellow dots marked on the street are. They mark the dead area where depressing the power pedal has no effect on forward traction.

So, if you see dots in the middle of the crosswalk, it means we have no power at this point. Shouldn't the breakers be placed in such a way that there are no dead areas at critical pedestrian and car crossings? *Thank you.* Now you are beginning to see things from a trolley man's point of view. The dead area placement is affected by where the power poles are positioned, which has much to do with trees, buildings, and numerous other obstacles. Take time to study an intersection, and notice what decisions went into why things are where they are. Eventually, you could graduate to an intersection like Church and Duboce or S. Van Ness and Mission. It isn't as simple as it seems at first, especially if streets come together at odd angles due to the city's topography.

## Surge Suppressors

On the leading edge of all crossovers is a thing that looks like an Oreo cookie perpendicular to the wires. It suppresses a spark from a depressed power pedal should an operator have power on when crossing a breaker. If you have ever been on an electric bus that shudders suddenly, this is because the operator has the power pedal depressed over a breaker. This occurs when trying to move in stopped traffic, especially uphill near a stoplight. If the dot on the street isn't measured correctly, or is worn away or unmarked, a jolt can be felt.

The surge suppressor reduces this jolt. It is a pair of insulated disks that try to suppress the flash from power attempting to short between the crossing wires. Sometimes, these become detached from the wires due to frequent jolts, and this causes trolleys to dewire near intersections and turns. It took me six months to get the surge suppressor fixed at the Townsend Caltrain crossover for the 45 Union. The glaze in the gaze of an inspector trying to guess what I had described over the radio told me nothing was going to get done. No one in street ops knew what a surge suppressor was. This compartmentalization between departments in the city is a hassle any small business person understands if trying to get a permit or pay a fee with the city. Can't we all get the kingdoms (departments) to talk to one another, and get along?

# Breakers

Of all crossovers and switches where opposing poles of electricity cross, the universal term breaker is used. This is all we are required to know as an operator of electric buses. A previous manager of the Overhead Division was asked to create a class plan to instruct new operators on the various parts of the overhead, but he retired before this plan was put into play. I try to get the names of the various parts of the overhead when I see the crew on break by a repair area, but this is not easy to do. Different guys on different crews may call a part by a different name. If I am moving through an area on a bus, or if I'm at a terminal and the crew is busy, it isn't all that common to get answers to questions about crossover parts and switches. Their general response is, "Did you call it in?" Rats. Okay, next time I have a problem in an area, I'll call it in. But not knowing the name of the part I see in need of repair makes it a challenge to use this part of my brain while driving. Hence, most operators don't make the call.

Nothing happens until more than two operators call in a dewirement problem. So I have to get my leader and follower to also make the call. This is not as easy as it sounds because we no longer see each other at the terminals due to recovery time cuts. Being on a racetrack means that if I want to communicate with my leader or follower, I have to be familiar with where our paths cross. I then have to get their attention and make sure they can hear me.

One of the first questions asked about inter-bus communication is the necessity to go through the OCC. We can't contact another bus directly. The best we can do is to get the cell phone number of our relief; we can then make a call at a terminal before relief time to let them know of a delay. Calling Central is the simplest and best way to make contact and should be the primary method of inter-bus contact. I have seen that "making deals" with another broke-down operator is usually too self-serving and not in the public's interest. Many times a coach's overload in going over a breaker occurs after the bus is hot and has been in service for several hours. A bus's performance changes as the day progresses. Power surges in the breakers have a lot to do with where a bus breaks down.

# Dog bone

In the middle of a converge or diverge is a set of opposing toggles that guide the collectors through a switch to make a smooth transition from one set of wires to another. Their pattern resembles the classic cartoon dog bone: two wide flanges at either end with a narrow middle. If they stick because of changing weather conditions like morning dew and fog, I ask for "special sauce" to be applied to reduce sticking. Sometimes, the toggles refuse to change or only go halfway. This causes dewirements at switches. The problem is the toggles may only act-up intermittently. This can cause a resource drain if an inspector is required to monitor a switch until observing a dewirement. As more coaches go through the area and it warms up, a switch may be okay. How a previous coach hit the dog bone can make a difference. Sometimes the dewirement only occurs after one coach makes a right turn preceding a straight-on coach or if a coach has worn shoes, bent collector, or a twisted pole. If my leader caused the problem by the way he or she went through, my follower may have no problem. This creates an awful cat-and- mouse waste of time. Inevitably, the switch needs to be fixed. I say, sooner than later, but it isn't up to me. Only inspectors can make the call. I have learned that even if nothing gets observed or fixed right away, I can relax by knowing I did the right thing. Leaving it up to *God's time* is a big resentment I needed to get over as a bus driver. In the meanwhile, it's three-to-five mph when crossing through special work.

# Pan

Above most inductive switches is a sheet metal piece referred to as a pan. It shields the transmitter ball located at the end of the right pole from sending its signal to other switches in the area. When new switches are installed, they are without a pan of metal over them to shield the signal. I went through a two-year battle to get pans installed over the inductive ring wired to turn the toggles in the switch, especially at North Point and Van Ness.

After countless dewirements, pans were installed. It is this poverty consciousness that pervades most government agencies, transportation notwithstanding. Waiting for failure is the watchword for trolley repair and overhead repair, and it is another battle in my head that I have to let go of if I am to stay safe. People ask me why I am writing this book, and this could be my number one reason.

I can't change the system, but I can change myself. And this alters the impression I am creating when behind the wheel of that large automobile. How did I get here? Sounds like talking heads, no? The new doughnuts are white and are not necessarily installed with a pan on top. Only after months or years of calls do they get a pan that shields the signal from another trolley. Cue Bob Dylan's *Blowin' in the Wind* as to when the switch will be installed properly.

Truth be told, some switches activate for no apparent reason. No matter how meticulous a pan is installed to shield a nearby trolley coach from inadvertent trigger, switches activate on their own. I have looked at my switch control dial in the normal position, only to see that the semaphore has changed, or I hear the click of the switch changing even before I am over the doughnut. As a line trainer, this is a mandatory lesson about what makes a trolley operator differ from a motor coach operator. We must listen to what the overhead is telling us, especially when we need to turn on a switch.

Fortunately, I am always aware of what position the switch is in before I cross the intersection. I have not brought down any overhead due to a falsely-triggered switch. As a line trainer, I tell my students where these ghosts are in the system. A study of the natural earth energy lines does make for a compelling reason as to why these electrical mysteries keep happening.

# Doughnut

Underneath the pan is the doughnut. This is the electromagnetic loop that sends the turn signal message from our foot pedal button on the floor to the switch. In certain areas, such as Main and Mission, Mission and 30th, and Market and Eighth, a following trolley must not activate a turn signal until the lead coach has passed the frog of the switch. Reactivating the toggles before the lead coach passes causes the lead coach to switch incorrectly. I am good at spotting this, and when my follower is in a rush, he has to then reset his poles due to the fact that the switch is now set in the wrong direction because he passed the doughnut. The distance between the doughnut and switch is too far away, and more than one trolley can pause between the transmitter and the diverge. Anyway, I haven't heard of drivers getting in trouble for this, but I think that they should. Call me *Mister Overhead*. If drivers follow the one block spacing rule, these dewirements would not occur.

The newer trolleys have a smaller footprint on the wires. The poles are two feet longer. Less metal is used and parts are more flexible. To be fair, these improvements have helped tremendously. New switches seem to have fewer problems, and all trolleys can get around a repair area using battery power. These changes have made for a nicer day behind the wheel.

# Selectric Switch

If you look up near an intersection of two trolley lines, you may see two staggered, parallel gray boxes before the converge of two sets of wires. These are selectric switches. They are triggered by the angle of the dangle. When a coach begins a turn, the poles begin to skew on track and are no longer parallel on the wires. The angle of the bus with the poles askew triggers the switch because the gray boxes are hit simultaneously by the angled poles. If you stand by such a corner, you can hear the click as a trolley makes a turn onto another line. Being in a Zen state means being able to hear the click.

# DROP AND RACK

In training, the coach securement is very clear. There are no passengers on board the bus, and no timetable exists. Usually the training coach is behind an in-service bus, and there are no other trolleys coming up from behind. The order from the training inspector to drop and rack the poles is given before lunch at the food court down at ferry plaza, and there is no pressure in how long this takes. Not so in revenue service. As any San Franciscan can testify, our streets are in a continual state of destruction, construction, and re-construction. Building demolitions are all over town as new high rise complexes go up. These sites usually have to block off the sidewalk and the one lane closest to the site.

This means the wires must first be moved over by the overhead crew in the big yellow truck, or it could mean diesel buses must pull out from another division. The third possibility is to "drop and rack" and battery power around. As I am writing this chapter, there is an extensive e.p.u. (emergency power unit) situation down near the foot of Market on Drumm Street to Sacramento Street. Inspectors are placed before and after the construction site to cradle our poles nearside, and replace them back on the wires after the area that has the wires completely removed. If you have ever seen those large excavation machines, attendant with their massive armature and bucket attachments, (cherry picker) you can quickly see why the wires must be turned off, moved, or in this downtown case, completely removed altogether. The risk of creating a ground short through the arm of the excavation machine can send a huge fireball and flash as the 600 volts of direct current travels between the two wires through the metal crossing.

The duty these inspectors have gives me sympathy, as the repetitive motion they must go through to place poles down and up over several hours could easily lead to injury. If I know a de-energized area is ahead, and I am in a convenient bus stop, that rolls downhill to the site, I cradle my poles uphill to give them a break, especially if many coaches are close together, or coming from more than one direction at one time. Sometimes they don't notice my poles are already cradled, and I get a kick out of their panic if they are not looking up, and then the smile and relief when they see they don't have to rack them.

Other than a smile from an inspector, comes the reading of the "riot act." This is a very intense scold about a rules infraction and the threat of: I could write you up. I was very taken aback by this, until an old timer told me that this verbal riot act is a friendly reminder that I probably won't be written-up because they are telling it like it is at the time I pass-by. It's a contra-indication like when we get the complaint from a passenger that is passive aggressive. The quiet ones that don't say anything are who you have to be wary of. Anyway, where was I? Oh yes, the order to drop and rack. In most cases we, the operator, must do this ourself. The posting of an inspector is a luxury.

To me, the key is to rack my poles far enough in advance of a downhill roll, so there is not the gridlock of stopping when other vehicles add to the problem. If I can smoothly transition the area without stopping, on the emergency power unit, then the flow is kept, and a back-up of cars are minimized or cleared. If uphill, I like to put my poles on the opposing wires and travel on the left side without using a battery. Any grade above 2 per cent really drains the battery, and some coaches are weaker than others. I try to communicate this status to any inspector in the area, but the chief complaint we have is that the inspector is not visible, or not standing in a position closest to where we need them to be. Inattentive police and fire crews cause minutes of delay where none need be if they understood our traveling limitations. Many times an ambulance or squad car need be parked or stopped just a few inches difference to make a lane available to us and our passengers.

In any event, the one block spacing rule becomes very apparent when a drop and rack situation exists. Also very important to take in to consideration is the notion of, if I should lose all my air, and be unable to move, can I use gravity or battery power while I still have it, to move to a space in parked cars or away from an intersection, to make it easier for others to pass by? An operator busy with getting people off of the bus, but with poles up on the wires, can make a bigger jam if following trolleys can not get around.

Even though the first rule of thumb is that the out-of-service vehicle should be the first one that has its' poles dropped and racked, I still act defensively by taking the offense, and rack my own poles, first. I can then go around the coach that has its' poles up, and let that operator drop them when they are of the mental capacity to do so.

A successful drop and rack is not is easy as it sounds, and when done smoothly and in timely fashion is a great way to keep the Zen inside the bus, and may result in applause once clear of delay!

Once the power went out at busy 16th and Mission and I immediately switched to battery power because I knew there was a separate power block on the other side of 13th. Sure enough, I passed all the other stopped trolleys and when I got through the three blocks of dead wire, the 600 volt hum returned. I had a wheelchair that needed to get downtown to 6th, and they made it without any delay.

The other operators stared with open mouths as they saw me fly by with poles up and on the wires, moving. The coach that day was one of the best for strong e.p.u., emergency power unit, and my speed was over ten mph. I love the cheers when we got back to power three blocks down. Here was a case when stopping all the buses was not really necessary. Knowing where the power blocks are helps keep the Zen when powerless!

# SERVICE DOGS

Or should I say service animals? All creatures, great and small, do we see on a day as an operator of trolleys. As a new operator, it takes getting used to all of the various creatures that qualify as service animals. I would like to see the permit of that pit bull or that boa constrictor, but we are *trained* by the blow-back from the owner not to question their integrity, lest we violate the rules of the Americans with Disability Act. And so we learn to nod and a smile to continue without disruption, until another passenger complains about safety being violated.

We are only allowed one nonservice dog per coach. If a small dog can be contained in the arms of a passenger, it is usually okay. But if another large dog enters that is a service dog, it has priority. Trained service dogs are expected to behave in a respectful manner. But some passengers are calling their dogs, *service* dogs that do not behave as I would expect a service dog to behave. Muni permits any number of service dogs on one coach, but I would expect their owners to be mindful of where they sit, especially if another dog comes on board. If you bring on a puppy, I would expect you to carry newspaper for any "accident." Hopping off the bus after a tinkle does not seem to be responsible, and I resent those who seem unaware of their effect on other passengers remaining on board. Car cleaning is not in my job description, but I have learned how to keep in service with extra newspapers.

# FAUX PAS NUMBER 117

For trekkers reading these entries, a similarity to the Ferengi text, *The Rules of Acquisition*, may become apparent. Containing over 200 *laws* of conduct with respect to financial decisions and actions, it is a sort of bible for this alien species. It is often quoted as a form of wisdom for maximizing profit in any encounter where a clear-cut answer may be difficult. So, too, do we have an unwritten (until now) code of conduct of how to ride a bus in San Francisco. Perhaps, in response to your curiosity and genuine interest in such matters, I may produce this sacred list for public view in a book or on my Facebook wall.

As you can see, the number 117 implies there are many such faux pas on board or around a coach, that lead to a less than desirable outcome of reaching your destination in a timely fashion. Oddly enough, with over sixteen years of service as a transit operator in this city, and with daily contact with hundreds of passengers and a multitude of friends and acquaintances, it never ceases to amaze me that almost no one is familiar with Muni faux pas. It may take a holy pilgrim to find a new law or rule of parts acquisition for the railway.

In Gene Roddenberry's world of *Star Trek*, the entire culture seems to be familiar with the rules of acquisition of an alien species within the federation. Here on present day earth in San Francisco, I have yet to encounter a single person versed on *The Dao of Doug: The Art of Driving A Bus*. There seems to be a complete cluelessness about Muni faux pas that prevents transit from running on time. Certainly the thousands of riders of Muni must wonder why this is so. Although I don't have Picard's clarity to make it so, I hope this helps.

Indeed, as voters are again asked to fund another proposition for bringing money into our transit system, it is clear that the many of this organization do not understand Ferengi's *The Rules of Acquisition*. I don't recall what number this rule is, but if you want to buy new buses for a riding public or provide timely parts replacement for its fleet, you do need to pay your bills on time.

This would include brushes and bushings for traction motors and doors and parts for airbags and wheelchair lifts to pick up those with mobility problems. If, in a voter pamphlet, you ask the public to fund the bus system with more parking meter money to "have a clean, safe, and reliable transit system our world-class city deserves," one would expect that the extra money would go to the bus transportation department. [See *The Examiner*, p. 4, April 14, 2013.] Work orders to other departments have given rise to a new nick name for the MTA's initials, ATM! Muni is a cash machine for other department budgets, especially if you keep promising the same thing over and over again, year after year with different propositions. Perhaps this ground-breaking dialogue can begin here with the mention of faux-pas 117.

Faux pas 117 is demanding to board a coach in a wheelchair, even after the operator suggests taking a following bus. As a bus driver, I am always concerned for your comfort. My suggestion to wait for the next coach is based on the experience of the condition of the equipment, the passenger load, the headway, and the weather and traffic. (These last two conditions are on the civil service test.) All these have their corresponding number on the faux pas list, but none seems as simple as 117, which is to simply wait for the next bus if your boarding requires use of the accessory power and secondary use of the AC inverter. Having to wait for a tow truck or for the shop can take up to forty minutes. If the shop arrives in twenty minutes and the repair person can't unstick your wheelchair from the lift or from inside the coach, another delay may exist in waiting for the tow truck guy to build air back up in the coach.

Listening to an operator's suggestion, even though it sounds contrary, may be the best course of action. We are all trying to make do and do the best we can with what we have been given. Parts are replaced on an emergency or crisis management basis. Good news is no news, except for spare parts. If a report appears in the paper about a door staying open, it is a good bet the brushes and rollers are on their way.

Sure enough, after a highlight of an open train door in the news, I have never had to call the shop for slow doors, doors that won't close, or pull in with doors that stopped working. In this case, bad news is good news. The money will be found to fix the problem. In the meantime, Zen is your best friend.

# ROLLING DELAY

Whenever we fall back five minutes from the checkpoint time on our paddle, we are supposed to call the OCC. Operations Central Control, or "Central," takes note of this and can switch us back for time and place. On trolleys, we have a turn-back on the wires (on average) for every twenty minutes of headway. We can save ten minutes off of our outbound terminal arriving time and gain another ten minutes as we face inbound ten minutes ahead of the outbound terminal. If it takes fifty minutes to complete a trip from point A to B, and we have at least two switchbacks to turn us around to get back on schedule, we can call for a switch.

But, as you can see, this does *not* work if we are only five minutes late. As Central has told me, such a switch, if only five down, results in too much time, that is, too much break time for the operator. Not to sound too argumentative over the air, I asked them what their definition of "too much time" meant. The answer: twenty minutes. Giving an operator twenty minutes off during a heavy trip is too much time. So, we learn that five minutes down results in no switch. Well, what about ten minutes? Nope. Fifteen? Almost always, no. This is where push comes to shove in the aisle and in the development of a rushed mentality in the operator's mind that has put the N Judah line into accident mode (with the same thing sometimes occurring on the 5 Fulton).

Many riders are familiar with the N Judah turn-backs on the way to Ocean Beach. These resulted, finally, in additional diesel shuttle service on NX motor coaches. Only after a barrage of serious accidents was reported in the news did this change. A current running time "shortage" exists on the 5 Fulton trolley as operators are pushing the pedal and abruptly braking along the path downtown and out to the ocean. (After posting this chapter on my Facebook page, I shortly heard that a 5 Rapid service was to begin. Sure enough, as I edit this chapter, we now have a 5 Rapid bus with new motor coaches servicing the area inbound from 6th Avenue, so those waiting at Masonic have an empty bus with seats available. Hurrah!)

When recovery time at the end of the line is cut, it makes for a rough ride. If you aren't holding on when the coach starts or stops, you can find yourself running into your neighbor. This may or may not be a bad thing, depending on who you are pressing up against. It is the topic of many blogs, but from a safety standpoint, this is not sustainable. And we as operators live with it. You, as passengers, also put up with it. I have to accept that any delay of less than twenty minutes is considered a rolling delay and may not result in a switchback to recover.

Anyway, I see a direct link with my troubles on the line with a lack of running and recovery time at the terminal. I can call in a twenty-minute personal necessity to get a mental or physical break, as is required by law, but this can also cause gaps in headway (the time between buses). And schedules have placed extra relief times in the middle of the day to force operators to make it to the relief point on time for relief. This discourages us from calling in a 702 (personal necessity), as we have to make relief with our coworker starting their shift. The idea, "I only have one more trip," does work to make for fewer call-ins, and keeps the buses moving.

So, a rolling delay (defined as any delay less than twenty minutes) makes for a challenge to start and end a shift on time. This is why many operators are choosing to work straight through. No reliefs in the middle of a shift, but either a pull-out or pull-in so that no conflict can arise with rolling delays in having to adjust for a relief time.

This is how our railway used to make the schedule. One run does one line, and you start and end your day on the line. You make one relief. You build rapport with the inspector on the corner, and you come to know your leader and follower.

Now, there are so many relief breaks during the day shift that, in my opinion, coupled with rotating days off, it creates less accountability than in the past. I think keeping it simple makes for a smooth schedule. Back in the day, one operator did one line with one relief time. Keeping Zen on the line is a good bet when the feedback from a departing passenger is a *thank you* for a smooth ride.

# BLOCKED ZONE

You can tell experienced operators by how they flag stop a blocked zone. Stopping at the top of the key so that the crosswalk is not blocked is a good first sign. Keeping the left lane clear is also good. Clearing the crossover on the overhead wires allows for a crossing transfer bus to pass through the intersection. This permits cars to pass by, even though the bus is not at the curb. The number one complaint from motorists is that the bus is blocking traffic while picking up passengers. I also try to get eye-to-eye contact with those intending, and point ahead to top of the zone so they know where to move to board the coach when blocked by another vehicle.

This happens frequently in the city. Charter or tour buses take up almost the whole zone. Delivery trucks' lift gates encroach upon the top of the zone. Taxis and personal vehicle boarding and drop-offs also block the zone, particularly if those passengers are not ready to disembark. Not ready because they are carrying something or don't have the money ready to pay the taxi driver. Suitcases or bags are very common in front of hotels or at BART stations. All this needs to be kept in the entire view of what is developing ahead of us as we make the decision about where to place our doors.

Sharing the zone with growing numbers of shuttle buses to accommodate an increase in tech company employees in Silicon Valley has led to some frustration and delay. If we, in our city trolley, need to pick up or deploy the lift for a wheelchair or senior needing assistance, this sharing can become a problem. Three hundred Muni stops were given permission for the Google, Facebook, Genentech, and Yahoo coaches to share with us. For one dollar, these Silicon Valley work shuttles were allowed to use our stops. This payment arose when those coaches were blocked by angry protestors lamenting the rent increases around such stops by the huge demand created by techies living in the city and working down south on the peninsula.

But in talking to a tech worker riding a Muni bus one night, I confirmed what I had learned from two friends who rode the Caltrain diesel conventional rail commuter line to points south and back. And the sticking point is, and always has been, that the "transfer costs" eat up time and money between transit agencies. These shuttle buses are "free" for employees, and are a one coach pick-up and drop-off, "nonstop" ride to and from work.

As a metro area, we have still failed in seamless connection between agencies, particularly to the south. An express 16AX, BX Muni line was cut off short of Caltrain, much to the dismay of those few loyal riders from the avenues to Soma and on to Santa Clara County, which we call Silicon Valley.

Santa Clara is one county south of San Mateo, the large county that borders San Francisco County, and it separates the city from the sprawling tech campuses of Apple, Cisco, Oracle, and the like. Though some campuses are in San Mateo County, one cannot transfer to points south from the city with a timed transfer and/or a single payment, except for using these free shuttles. The sad thing is that our Caltrain infrastructure did not improve with express service from residential areas around San Francisco to a train line that also suffers from abrupt closings due to fire, pedestrian collision, and blocked tracks. Access is all too easy to the rail right-of-way, and fencing and grade improvement are, and have been, long overdue.

The ease with which a policy change can occur from a single protest is amazing. For over three years, we operators gradually became familiar with these Silicon Valley tour bus coaches; over time, we have smoothed out most of the zone-sharing problems.

Talking and sharing in the Gilley (break) room helped us deal with the frustration and close calls in getting used to the shuttle drivers on our line, especially the 24 and 49. No mention was ever made of any help in extending zone curb clears for zone sharing or fines or fees when we had a line delay. Only with public protest did any acknowledgement come from city government. But, as with most problems, we had already dealt with it in the Gilley room, as with all the other blocked zone problems that we face daily.

Keeping Zen in transit means I signal to you where I am going to stop. It also helps that you recognize I am a person driving a bus, and not just a bus.

# ONE BLOCK SPACING

One of the things about trolleys is that our poles can block the vehicle behind us when they are up and we are out of service. If another coach is not observing the one block spacing rule and follows the leader into the zone where that coach goes out of service, conflict can arise in waiting for the leader to pull poles and clear the wires for the second bus to pull around the out-of-service bus. If I see a bus in a crowded zone, I now almost always wait to see if the left turn signal goes on, the doors close, and the bus begins to move. I have been burned one too many times when the bus in front finished loading and then goes out of service.

Being a Muni bus driver forever changes how we stop behind another vehicle. The division instructor's reminder to always leave enough of a space cushion in front of us to pull around any vehicle in the zone becomes painfully clear when our leader secures the coach. The distraction and safety rules in handling a situation on the bus can mean that the operator cannot go to the back of the bus and cradle the poles. Staying back behind the crosswalk on the nearside of an intersection is an ace in the hole when this happens. It gives us pause to determine what action to take next without being blocked in.

In one of the few times I have received multiple passenger service requests (PSRs) or complaints about my service, it has been when my leader has been dragging, falls back on my time, has a completely full coach, and has a security incident which requires securing the coach. In such a situation, before she can leave the cockpit to rack the poles, it may be necessary for her to complete a call for help on the radio or to wait until a security incident onboard clears before leaving the seat. This delay is variable, and by waiting to cross by one light cycle, I am giving her time to see me in her rear view mirror. My toot of the horn or flash of high beams can be a good signal to confirm she sees that I am ready to cross behind and unblock the wires.

In these times, stepping off to secure and rack her poles may be the best course of action, even though I may not be able to see her directly. In the case in point, I had waited nearside at the extremely wide intersection of Market and Van Ness and noticed she was not moving. Her coach was loaded, but she was not moving for one full traffic light cycle. I knew by waiting nearside that something was up. My delay to cross Market and stop behind her coach was just long enough that she came to the back and racked her poles. I also heard from her that she did have a security incident and was waiting for help. I had stopped far enough back to go around. This bus zone is long enough for two sixty foot trolleys, so I knew I had enough room when I crossed. A flag stop is also another great way to let a driver know I am right behind and ready to take on his/her passenger load.

But there are major transfer points, such as at 16th and Mission outbound, where there is not enough room for two long coaches. Failure to wait for a coach to finish boarding before crossing over to the far side is a violation of the one block spacing rule, but there seems not to be much enforcement of this rule. The second coach hangs back into the crosswalk, and the poles do not clear the crossover for the wires of the outbound 22 Fillmore. I have been blocked several times while I am on the 22, and as soon as Mission is blocked, traffic backs up as those in the right lane cannot make a right turn. Lucky is the day when motorists realize they can proceed forward one-half block to Capp to make a right turn there. The Mission has the best San Francisco motorists because they adapt quickly to Muni buses blocking the lane.

This has happened several times this sign-up as I work the 22 Fillmore. Because the second coach on Mission did not observe the one block spacing rule, the wires on the Mission and on 16th are blocked; he followed the 14 R into the zone which then went out of service.

When I am the lead coach of two buses at this transfer stop, I pull beyond the bus bulb, though still in the red curb clear zone, and give enough room for a follower. Flagging it to the left if a produce truck is unloading always helps. I make sure there are no wheelchairs or walkers in the zone before I make this decision to flag it.

Also important at these major transfer points is to look left and right to see if a 33 is intending to turn into the zone behind the outbound 16th and Mission bus zone. The 33 would also do well to look left and see if a 22 is ready to depart outbound from the other side of the intersection. A skilled 33 operator can cut short to allow the 22 to pass. The same goes for 18th and Mission, whereby the 33 can move up far enough in the zone to let another bus come in behind inbound on the Mission. And Mission operators can look left at 18th when heading inbound to see if a 33 is intending to follow them into the zone.

Of course there are times when teaching a lesson becomes critical for getting the message of safety across and not over the radio. If a coach stops short in the zone, denying space for the follower to enter the intersection, it is a nonverbal communication to slow down and give me space. Follow me at a distance. If the first attempt to stop the follower from tailgating fails, and the second bus is blocking the cross street while I attempt to off-load a wheelchair, this delay in moving should be enough to get the message. If not, I can wait at a stale green and cross after the amber to prevent the follower from crossing. If this still fails and they still follow, then it is time to pull my poles. If it means that much to you, then go! I guess this could be the ultimate time to go out of service—back in the zone, just clearing the crosswalk to secure the poles. Many times the Muni gods intervene, and the lead bus stops working. The complaint falls upon the follower, not the leader. This is a convenient way to serve paperwork without ever having to file a miscellaneous or call Central. Keeping the Zen means observing the one block spacing rule.

# THE FLAG STOP

At certain places, even though a buttonhook turn is the textbook style for making a right turn, there are those intense corners where the simplicity of the flag stop becomes the default stop. This is so because of intending transfer passengers, late to the cue, who wish to board from the crosswalk and expect the door to reopen. I repeat. They expect the door to reopen after the "train" has left the "station."

O great Buddha. O angels and archangels and all the company of heaven. SaLuSa, Metatron, Hilarion, St. Germaine, Jesus the Christ, Galactic Federation, The High Council of Orion, The Andromeda Council, The Council of Twelve, all ascended masters, all light workers, and all way-showers, to all do I pray.

As do my brethren behind the wheel of a Muni bus in San Francisco and those who watch the contrasts we experience every day. Let the riding public know that there are traffic considerations, the beat, the pulse of the city that can create a delay in reopening the front door. For it is sometimes not just for one that the door cannot be reopened. It is for all those who see that the door is open and come from all directions. It is the shuttle or zip car that cannot wait for two seconds that pull around from the left and block the door as they attempt to turn right.

It is the buttonhook created by other vehicles that adds to another light cycle and to a repeat process of the same expectation in waiting for the next light. For you see, the longer we do not move, the more who will enter. And at Union and Columbus, on our 9:00 a.m. trip, the bus is full. At 16 and Mission on any weekday or weekend afternoon, the bus is full. Alleluia. Praise prime creator!

Other, less congested corners have the same unsafe dynamic, even though pedestrian traffic is "manageable." Outbound 16th and Kansas is usually a buttonhook right, but the delay in pulling away from the curb has cars blocking us from the left or main traffic lane. The same is true for turning right onto 3rd from 18th. If we flag the stop, we don't have to worry about the threat from behind and to the left.

Even with sixteen years under my belt, I still needed help with this, as I was getting complaints from those walking from the 30 Stockton who wished to transfer to the 41. The reason some operators refuse to do the 41 is primarily because of this transfer at Columbus and Union. The added variable is an intersection right behind the bus at Powell. A car or truck can come out of nowhere right behind us on Powell and attempt a right to go around us in their search for parking.

This is where the thought occurs that folks looking for parking slow down transit. Even if we successfully block them from blocking us on a buttonhook, they may still speed ahead, only to double-park and attempt to back into parallel parking on the curb. I would have to say that this is the biggest challenge to surrender built into the job as a transit operator— rushing cars or intending passengers who expect to "get ahead" while we, behind the seat, are trying to prioritize safety.

We would rather risk a complaint than fill out an accident report, but this is little comfort when sitting in a complaint hearing. Could we really prove that we are saving ourselves from the accident, the contact with another vehicle or person? This truly is in God's hands. All we can do is say, "Oh well." Amen. Peace be with you!

# READING ON MUNI

Being able to read on Muni is probably an art form. Maybe it will be a new X-game or reality show. A built-in announcement on our digital voice activation system (D.V.A.S.) states, as soon as we close the door, is, "Please Hold On." On to 'what' has been open to conjecture. "Dear Life" may be the number one response to a recently polled riding audience. But just as we operators appear to master the incomprehensible act of driving a bus in San Francisco with plenty of bozos, so too can our riders master feats of derring-do just like any superhero. Reading on Muni can actually be mastered. As can texting or typing on a computer. My hat is off to you stalwart heros that can multi-task while riding an electric trolley bus.

I read newspapers when I take the bus in the morning. No problem. The coach is quiet and relatively empty. But trying to read in the afternoon is much more difficult because of the noise and limited space. If two passengers are engaged in a heated debate, or someone is on their cell phone with attitude about their mate or friend not behaving in a way that is suitable to them, this all becomes public knowledge. Trying to ignore these heated conversation blasts is next to impossible.

Most of my friends have told me that this is why they don't ride Muni anymore. "If you could just get rid of these 'boundary crossing' crazies, I might give the bus a second chance. Most riders, no matter how rude or loud they act towards other passengers, are usually kind and gracious to the operator. So how we deal with the battle of wills between two passengers becomes not unlike a UN Council of Nations, or such as in an envoy sent from the embassy! Restating the needs of each party helps, as does the person who was 'first' in disrespect and why. But it is hard to come up with any hard and fast rules on paper. Only with the months turning in to the years, with a repeat of a similar situation, can matters be dissolved quickly. Just when I think I have it, another twist occurs, and reveals more.

Keeping Zen means not taking things personally and starting fresh every day.

# THE PA: CALLING OUT STOPS

Only a small percentage of the ETI Skoda coaches have volume set correctly. I have been told that problems arising from the DVAS module are due to a bad chip. The shop's mantra upon pull-in at the tower is that these are checked and replaced every six months on all coaches. This provides little assurance. Rather than fix the problem on a daily pull-in basis, this defect is passed on months down the line, and no specific defects on the module are corrected.

The DVAS module is the communications lifeline. It sends information about where the bus is and links with passengers' telephones and the bus shelter clock to update information about how long it will be before arriving at the intended location. The inconvenience caused by not getting this information makes a big difference if headway is longer than ten minutes (such as at night or early morning) and can affect what kind of day I have. Are you running helplessly to the bus stop because I am arriving sooner than the clock time? Are you leaving the stop because the next bus says I have departed?

Not having a working mic or one that distorts, really slows things down and creates bad blood about flag stops, pull-ins, and emergency vehicles or construction delays. Half of my passenger service complaints would go away if my coach had a functional DVAS and properly-calibrated mic control.

There is space on the DVAS announcement cue for up to ninety-nine announcements. *Shake your umbrella outside, wheelchair boarding, wheelchair coming out,* would all be great announcements. Short destination announcements when we have a switchback or are pulling in that would announce, *This is the last stop,* would also be helpful. The number 6 had this announcement at Market upon inbound pull-in, but it was dropped. This underutilization is another example where operators' skill and experience are going unused on the DVAS system.

One secret I have found that most other operators never seem to get is that about a third of the incorrectly calibrated mic volume controls can be minimized by turning down the volume to a one, two, or three level and using a low tone of voice. When first taking over at a relief point, if the DVAS allows, I scroll down the volume and click to the outside speaker.

I test the level to see if I can hear myself clearly. If the call-out sounds distorted, I know not to keep the speaker control on "inside" or "both." This way, even though my rhythm or habit is to depress the floor button to call out a stop, I won't shock or overwhelm those inside with an awful howl or static if I hit the call-out button. The button is on the floor near the turn signals and high-beam buttons.

Because I am in the habit of using this button, there are times when I depress the button out of habit, forgetting that the bus I currently have doesn't have a clear signal. I sometimes have to force my *second nature* self to call out stops without using a PA. If the coach is really crowded, it is impossible for everyone to hear a call-out, but as long as I am making an effort, I won't get into trouble.

The rule to call out stops does not specify how loud or soft the announcement should be or whether or not everyone can hear it. This comes into play when a spotter is on board the bus observing us to see if we call out stops. I am always aghast when I get written up for not calling out stops because I have such conscientious awareness about it. This is when I become angry about the shop dismissing such defects as inconsequential, as this will be "fixed" on a rotating, semi-annual basis.

This is one of the primary reasons we, as operators, stop filling out defect cards; we see no change or correction from the shop. We guess as to what gets done, and eventually we are "trained" not to put defects down on the card when we pull in.

Rebooting the coach does help in making DVAS problems go away, so if I can find the correct time and place to turn off my coach, I do. But whether or not this will work is also a problem. Sometimes I believe volume control is changed remotely if someone is listening in on camera from a laptop at a mobile location or downtown. This is the only explanation I have as to why volume control changes in mid-trip. Other times, there are freezes on controls, and our bus position does not move on the stop request. The clock can read a different time, or the bus stop request bell stops working. These computer chip-related challenges make for a frustrating day. We never know if we are being recorded or if or when our PA will be restored.

This is when our diary book comes in handy. We can write down the coach number and defect when we have such a bus. If a complaint comes in for not making an announcement, we have our "black book" ready with the defects of the day. Saving our white copy of the defect card goes a long way toward keeping the Zen while driving a trolley with a computer card for stop requests and PA control.

# VTT

This is why a bus driver, particularly a trolley man or trolley woman, is usually the last motorist stuck in traffic to talk about your mama. We are the professionals! We give turn signals well in advance, know proper use of the horn, and change lanes in advance of hazards a block away. Operators have a better vantage point than those of you in cars. Motorists would do well to follow a city bus through a single lane detour or straddling a lane. We know how to trail-blaze, and we will let you see ahead of us as soon as the next bus stops at the next light. We also have signal preempts, which means we keep the light green longer than normal to allow us to keep the green on for you when you follow us. Our buses communicate with those traffic lights that have a small white panel located on the mast arm of the overhead signals. This is a great use of GPS-style technology, and our director of transit notifies us of such improvements.

The rush by cars to cross the yellow line or to get around at a four-way stop is just *cray-cray*. And this unsafe action seems to be happening more frequently, as does the attempt to pass when we are in a long cue of traffic waiting at a stop or a red.

So it is the VTT (Verified Transit Training) card we possess next to our license and our medical certificate that places us at the professional level on the road. We take classes on a regular basis to be reminded of how to handle the public on a city bus.

These classes are led by a state-certified safety instructor who often asks probing questions about various scenarios or has a senior operator answer questions from junior operators.

Unlike the informal conversations in the Gilley room back at the barn, the discussions usually begin with a video or training film. Accident review is similar, but the conversation is usually a round robin of the description of events or conditions leading up to an accident or a passenger complaint.

Though to some this may seem boring or pointless, I do always try to see if I can gain a new tidbit or helpful technique from someone else in these sessions. I usually do. How to adjust the windows to reduce the smell of a stinker was a biggie. Leaving a small crack open behind me helped with the crosscurrents. Thank God for the fog! Placing the doors for a flag stop at certain locations and the art of the making the radio call were all juicy tidbits I would not have discovered on my own.

For example, when calling in on-air about a problem location, I discovered it was clearer to just describe location and position of where the event happened instead of my current position. The delay in a message acknowledgement was a variable that I did not have to mention at the start of a call. I could always restate my location as I ended the call, thus keeping it simple for Central to copy.

When to call was also a great bi-product of VTT class. Calling during afternoon rush did not result in a quick response from Central, but calling during early morning hours did. There's also the art of when to call for a switchback. I was calling in too early. The shift change of the shop for a road call, the acceptance of a variable end time, and how to handle late-runners were all great points I learned at a VTT class. The list goes on.

And in AR or accident review, I learned the basic food groups of accidents and could see that contact made with the coach was either SSL, sideswipe left, SSR, sideswipe right, SP, squeeze play, TBR, TBL, T-bone right or left, and RE, rear end. Certain mirror positions also come into play for each line. Once I got my mirrors just right for each type of traffic, I stopped getting into trouble. Having mirrors high on the way to Daly City is not the same as going downtown on the 1 with mirrors down and close.

Crosstown 22 Fillmore has different mirror settings and style of driving than the 24 Divisadero, even though they are only five blocks apart in Western Addition. The 24 travels along a four-lane street and has long stretches without boarding in a residential area. The 22 is all about the art of the stop at the curb and saving the knees. In my opinion, the 22 is closest to the 1 California, and the 5 Fulton is much like the 14 Mission. The 49 seems to be in a class by itself. The fact that you do the Mission and then turn onto Van Ness is intense. To keep the Zen on the 49 requires taking a full ten at North Point, even if arriving late. Amen!

# RANGE SHEETS

Posted in the Gilley room at our bus barn are the range sheets. These are the shift schedules that tell you when you report, pull out, make relief, go on break, begin your second part, and finish. The second part is usually only on certain day shift assignments or runs. Most early starting or late starting runs are straight through. The general pattern of the runs on the range sheets goes as follows.

First are straight through runs that pull out in the early morning and get relieved after lunch. These begin as early as 4:00 a.m. and go to 1:00 p.m. or 2:00 p.m. There is no pull-in, so you may finish somewhere other than at the bus barn from where you pull out. The next set of work shifts are split day shifts. These runs start a little later in the morning, from 6:00 a.m. or 7:00 a.m., have a two-hour break in the middle, and then work until 6:00 p.m. or 7:00 p.m. Their range is twelve hours. Hence, the name of the sheets—range sheets. They give the shift range per run.

A sample line on the range sheets looks something like this:

| 676 | *6:36 | 1408 | 707/11:52(SR12:02) |
|-----|-------|------|--------------------|
|     | 505>2:02 | 602 | 6:36** |

Reading across, this says, Run 676 pulls out at 6:36 a.m. and is the eighth bus out on the 14 line or train 1408. At 11:52 a.m., the operator of run 707 is waiting for you at 11th and Mission inbound to relieve you. You get paid an extra ten minutes. Then, after lunch, you meet run 505 on the 6 line at 2:02 p.m. outbound. You pull in at 6:36 p.m.

The range sheets show the columns of pay that are not just platform time. Platform time is the time spent in the chair. Other forms of pay listed here are lunch, stand-by detail (SD), stand-by report (SR), travel time (TRAV), and overtime straight (OT),and overtime night (OT after 6 p.m.). Lunch has been cut from several runs posted on a new sign-up and equals twenty minutes.

Stand-by time used to total almost one hundred hours a day for all Potrero runs, but now it is less than five hours a day. This looks good in cutting payroll costs, but I believe this cut can actually lead to longer-term staffing problems in finding enough bodies to fill all these runs. Running time between check points on our paddles and recovery time at the end of the line also gets chopped, so that platform time becomes a challenge to make ends meet, especially without a switchback.

The other forms of pay become less accurate when buses are missing, as any regular rider can attest. Travel time takes longer to get to another relief point in heavy traffic. Stand-by detail accounts for those waiting in the Gilley room to be detailed at the last minute if another coach needs to be taken to a relief point as a coach trade. Stand-by report usually is for those operators taking over an open run that has not been detailed by the regular operator. They stand by on report waiting for the dispatcher to call their cap number over the PA. OT and night shift differential are other extra types of pay shown on the range sheets. OT starts after eight hours, and night shift begins after 6:00 p.m.

After these middle-of-the-day runs come early twilights. They start around 2:00 p.m. to 4:00 p.m. and go straight through with a pull-in around 9:00 p.m. Late twilights start after 4:00 p.m. and go as late as 2:00 a.m. Then comes the owls, which may start around dinnertime or 5:00 p.m. and go through till almost dawn or after an inbound, early-to-work run.

The great thing about all this is the diversity of start and finish times one has, as with days off. Days off are connected and paired in any combination of days off: weekends are Saturday and Sunday and then Sunday/Monday, Monday/Tuesday, Tuesday/Wednesday, Wednesday/Thursday, Thursday/Friday, and Friday/Saturday. Sunday/Monday and Friday/Saturday are very popular as a number-one choice in days off other than weekends.

Choices are made by seniority in three-minute-bid windows on the day of the sign-up that falls on your seniority rank, with the other operators at your barn for a barn signup, or system-wide for a general signup.

The distribution of days off is not equal. The number of days off for weekends isn't the same as for weekday days off. Monday/Tuesday or Tuesday/Wednesday may be the fewest groups of days off, with Thursday/Friday being the greatest number of days off. This can have an effect on those of us with lots of seniority with weekends off because it means that if we have a junior operator in front of us with days off in the middle of the week, his/her days-off may not get covered by the dispatcher. This has the same effect as an open run, so we are less sure of who, if any, will be in front of us and what our headway will be. So thinking that seniority means easier headway and fewer gaps between buses, may not be so.

For example, I call Central for a line check. This is the professional way to ask for help. It took me years to call calmly and use the correct language to request help on the radio. And then the hard part was to end the call quickly and with thanks. With an operator out for five weeks in front of me, the risk of complaints against me goes up.

The first week without a leader, Central did not acknowledge a problem. The dispatcher could say all runs were out, and this would be true at the start of my second part. What they weren't telling Central was that a car parker or early report person reaches maximum hours and pulls in early. This creates a triple headway situation that can extend for over four hours.

By the second week, Central said they would check, and after a pause, allowed me to move up five. By the third week, they would call and ask me to move up five. And by the fourth week, I checked the daily detail in the morning and saw a blank by the runs that were in front of me. This is where doing a great job without complaining seems unfair, in that the dispatcher fills holes with squeaky wheels.

The dispatcher is telling me not to stress out second desk by putting in for premium pay for not having a leader. I say that her stress is nothing compared to four-to-six hours of no leader on the 22 in the afternoon. We are entitled to extra run pay if we are working without a leader, but it has to happen for more than two consecutive days and for at least two hours or more in a shift.

Today, I can do this with a smile on my face. It would be my expectation to dismiss the chit of a safety warning, but the caution and reinstruct for a rescheduled conference still hangs in the air like ripened fruit needing to be picked. This is the emotional constitution we must have to stay at the job. We have to let things go and know that all we have to give to change a situation is love and not anger. Acceptance is the answer and the key to not falling into the bog of being a victim behind the wheel.

I have found working weekends to be much more relaxing than, say, working on a Tuesday. Having weekends off may not be such a great thing after all. And by working a twilight shift with two weekdays off, I have found I can schedule doctor or dentist appointments with ease and without having to resort to a run trade or time-off in the middle of the week. Indeed, finding a great block or run with weekdays off could be one solution to keeping the Zen at work on a trolley in San Francisco.

# RELIEF TIME

As mentioned in Rolling Delay, the day shift has an extra set of relief points to accommodate what is called a split. A split is a day shift run, in two parts, with a break in the middle of two hours off for lunch. Those of us who live in the city usually are the first to pick a day run split shift. I like this, as I find straight through runs can get me mentally or physically drained after the five hour mark in the seat has come and gone. A six hour part is too long a block, unless there is enough recovery time at the end of the line to use the restroom, eat something, stretch or make a phone call. I have learned that over six hours behind the wheel in a straight through, or on a second part of a split, has my body complaining, and that my mouth can become a liability with other passengers.

On the range sheets posted in the Gilley room, are four sets of symbols which let us know when we start and stop on our split. Back slash means inbound relief. Greater than symbol means outbound relief. This helps us know which side of the street to stand on at meeting our bus. Relief points are listed in the receiver's office where we pick up our paddles: our transfers and our checkpoint schedule for our run. A single star designates pull-out from the bus barn. Two stars mean we pull-in to the barn, and will not have to meet another operator at a relief point. Many operators favor this schedule, because there is no dependence upon another's schedule to work our run.

Relief time at relief points does add the characteristic of a Russian roulette when filling out a choice slip during a General Sign-Up. I try to find a split day shift that has two equal parts, with the second part hopefully being shorter. Five hours in the morning and four and a half in the second is ideal. Except than when it is not. Sometimes, time does seem to pass by faster in the morning than in the afternoon. A busy trip can make time pass by faster. It is a fine mental and spiritual and physical balancing act that becomes not unlike the ballet of life. At some point I have to let go and let God be the dancer. My will gets me in to a rock and a hard place. Better to look out over Alcatraz from the 41 line at Leavenworth on Russian Hill on a beautiful sunlit morning, then be assigned to "the rock" in a hard place on a seat that loses air and will not adjust!

The answer to the question at relief, "Is this a good one?" can be like carrying a loaded weapon. The response, "The coach runs smooth," means no flat tire, hard steer, or good braking. But oh, by the way, your mirrors shake like a wooden roof shingle in a wind storm, and you will find your butt on the floor as the chair slowly looses air on the way to Daly City! Hey, but it isn't safety significant. Really?

Keeping Zen means keeping quiet! Especially on a Friday on the last trip! Sometimes the best relief is a pull-in! No one to ask, "Is this coffee cup yours?" "Are these your papers?" Some operators build a nest around them when they occupy the seat for many hours, and it takes some doing to ask them to leave the coach as they found it. One can only wonder what their closet or kitchen looks like at home! "Get your stuff out of here!" may not be the best bet to start the day at relief!

# SLIDING SEATS

Sliding Seats is a term Greyhound bus drivers use when changing operators. The phrase at Muni is making relief. I like the Greyhound term because that is how making relief feels. Many mid-day or twilight shifts begin at a relief point somewhere along the line, and not as a pull-out from the barn. We meet our bus and our coworker at the relief point. We slide seats as one shift ends and another begins.

This is actually one of the great things about being a bus driver. Most of the time we are in our own "boat." Captain of the ship so to speak, and we don't have to deal with office politics or the personality of our coworkers. The brief encounter we have sliding seats is the only contact we have with our brethren, and usually a comment about the condition of the bus is all that is said. Usually. Sometimes it takes an heroic effort to get the bus to the relief point without going out-of-service. If our relief is bringing the bus late, it helps if they have already called Central Control to ask for, and receive, a switchback. Also, if a defect such as slow doors, no ring for a stop, or jammed fare box (which are not considered safety significant) can still be such a continuos intermittent distraction over a long shift, these defects can erode an operator's well being and lead to a passenger complaint.

This is where the diplomacy between coworkers has to be swift and concise. The more senior an operator, the easier to deal with and overcome a problem with the bus. On the other hand, some operators place ending the shift on time as a higher need than dealing with a problem on the bus. If a bus has a problem, the rules call for securing the coach and waiting for the shop. This means a missed relief. I can be at the relief point and no bus comes. And this is where the rules can be a hinderance or a help in keeping the headway stable with minimal disruption to service. We wait on the curb at the relief point until we see the run and bus behind us (our follower) pull up. This operator can tell us if they saw our bus on the side of the road. We can then call the OCC (Operations Central Control) to ask for orders. This is when a cell phone comes in handy. We can also use the radio of the late bus, but this causes delay on a bus that now has no leader.

Should we wait for our bus, or go back to the barn and pull out with a new bus? Only through the trial and error of coach defects, missed relief, time and location of relief, and OCC's orders, do we get a clearer picture of what to do when our bus is late or does not come at all.

Dispatchers can play a huge role in how smooth a transition day shift moves to twilight based on filling open runs on the extra board, or choosing a standby report operator to detail to a twilight run. Will they allow the operator standing-by enough time to get to the relief point to keep my leader in service? Or will that bus pull in, and then have a trip without a leader, only to hope a second coach pulls out later? Nowhere is this more important than on the 24 Divisadero, where the relief point is 20 minutes away from the barn, and is at a point in the middle of the line.

Potrero Barn is sweet in that inbound coaches can pull in without missing a beat if the second cut-in coach can pull out outbound, without too much drama or delay in headway. Not so with the 24. If on a day run sign up with a twilight leader in an open run situation, the last day shift trip can really be a trip. The problem is that this is occurs when people want to get home, and it is after many hours of being behind the wheel. Keeping Zen with a missed relief leader, a leader that is pulling in, is critical in being able to keep a day on schedule from falling apart. I would get so upset and take things personally.

Finally, it wasn't until I heard the same horror stories from other operators that I realized the best way to treat missed relief was to eye the detail sheet for missing names, and ask the dispatcher in advance at lunch if run blah blah blah was an open run, or working. Hopefully, if they connected a body to the hole in headway, I might stand a better chance of early notification of a move up, and keep the Zen!

# GSU

The term GSU is used often by operators when a system-wide sign-up occurs every other year. This is when bus drivers can change mode from diesel motor coaches to trolleys, from streetcars to cable cars, or move to bus barns at a different location. GSU stands for General Sign-Up. One of the things that makes Muni a cool job is in the flexibility to change shift, days off, mode, and location of where you go to work. Very few jobs allow this. Many a conversation about what my job is like when I get asked questions while in uniform stem from the topic of job benefits. For me, the flexibility of shift, start and end time, and location of work is sweet because it adds variety and flexibility.

Seniority is one of the issues that rarely come up. But, during a sign-up, knowing who you are talking to becomes important. Sometimes, without warning, recovery time is reduced from a line and run. And the standby and or travel pay of the run in front of you is modified so as to make for more or less time, which can have an effect of the seniority level of who chooses a run.

If someone tells me a run is no good, but they have signed onto it for more than three consecutive sign-ups, then I know it must be a good run or a run that works for them. They have less seniority than I do and don't want to lose their run to me. Or if someone says a run is really fantastic, but they never sign onto it, they may want to do the run I currently have. Looking at their cap number on the shoulder says it all. Are they ahead of me or after me in the sign-up?

Another trick is to look at the choice slip of those in front of me before they sign. Good ideas about runs I forgot to check come up fast. Others after me, dismayed at finding choices taken, look to see what my second choice is so they can go for that open run. This is when it gets down to less than five minutes before my sign-up time. But as I move up the seniority roster, run choices have less drama or politics than when days off and pay were more of a competitive challenge.

I love the barn I work out of because it dovetails nicely with my personal schedule, and the personalities of the other coworkers are easy-going and fun to be around. The shared experience we have together seems to form a bond not unlike that of US Marines who have been in battle together.

Because I have settled into the familiarity of my barn, I see little reason to change. The friendly and sometimes hilarious banter between us in the Gilley room keeps me energized to do good work and keeps me from my only remaining enemy, complacency.

Keeping the Zen means remaining in the same barn during a GSU. Familiarity with the cast of characters of passengers and operators makes for a job I enjoy showing up for on a daily basis.

# STOP SIGN AND THE FOUR-WAY STOP

The new, sleek design of late-model vehicles has one serious problem. That's the inability during daylight hours to see if a left turn signal is on at a four-way stop. Regulations requiring the turn signal cover to be amber fell away years ago. True, the bulbs inside most front side turn signals are still amber, but the curved cowling and slope of the turn light housing has a silver background, so during the day, it is more of a challenge to see if a vehicle is crossing an intersection or turning into the oncoming lane.

Most motorists are quick to cross an intersection at a four-way stop, but the lack of a turn signal requires that I wait to see them cross before I proceed. Often, it looks like they are crossing from right to left, and I am clear. Many times, they are coming left in front of me, and I cannot see their signal until after they are past the half-way point in the intersection.

This brings up a major pet peeve I have about some motorists. Was the intersection clear before you entered? Most sideswipes and T-bone contact could be avoided if the vehicle entering the intersection waited for the clear. When motorists delay using their signal, it also creates conflict that could be dramatically reduced and is the primary difference between a professional Class A or B driver, and a Class C motorist. "Oh yeah, I remember when I had a Class C license," implying less skill and knowledge, in a tone of sarcasm as a quick response on the exterior PA, followed by their response of a screech (burning rubber) at the window at the next red light. True, this is not a professional act on my part, but it is a fun way to let off steam, unless they get out of the car and come towards the bus. Oops, too much fun.

So, in order to keep the Zen, I must remember to pray for them what I wish for myself. This comes in handy when a pedestrian jaywalks, or a car fails to yield right-of-way. I remember back to when I did the same thing, and this helps my anger. I try not to flash to that image of strangling their neck. If I can take a deep breath or get a line of support from a passenger, all is well, at least for a little while. And Gina G. *Ooh, ooh, Just a Little Bit,* blaring from a nearby car radio never hurts.

# NOT MY FIRST RODEO

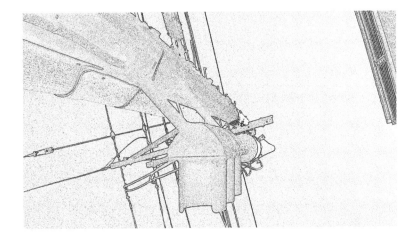

Dents and dings notwithstanding, one can tell how much time one has behind the wheel by looking no further than the defect card after making relief. Senior operators can roll with whatever they have been given. Others take safety to levels seen only at the National Security Agency. The biggest variable in accepting equipment is the personality and style of the person behind the wheel. We have terms for the style of movement an operator has during his or her run. I have a reputation as a runner. With Mars in Aries and my ascendant house rising in Leo, I have a charismatic demeanor that may come across as nondiplomatic, though I love to show my sunny side. In training, the only hint at personality is within the three points affecting safety: weather, traffic, and operator. This is an answer on the civil service test that can be remembered by the acronym WTO.

When I ask a mom with a screaming or crying baby to move back, other passengers in the rear react in shocked disbelief that I would ask a mom and baby to move back, leave the coach, or wait for the next one. Once again, it is O for operator. My sense of driving safely cannot be judged by another. I am driving a ten-ton vehicle in heavy rush hour traffic, and yes, any number of noises can be distracting, such as a relationship break-up over a cell phone, using the metal stanchions as a drum set, arguing about a deal, where to buy a product, and a whole assortment of other goodies.

Anyway, I see how what may be a good schedule during one sign-up can become a set-up for failure in another, depending upon the headway between transfer coaches, leaving time of a leader, and how fast one can push stale greens. I have learned to eat fresh greens, and this pause at a stoplight has turned my style into that of being a good guy. A good salad dressing also helps with kale. *Bada boom!*

By stopping well behind the crosswalk or stop line and looking at the "show" on the street, all is calm; all is well. Turk, Eddy, Post, Harrison, and Kansas are streets (just to name a few) where I do a self-check-in to see if I am pushing ahead or laying back.

The space cushion we are seen observing by driving down the hash mark of a two-lane street is actually a safety method which pays dividends at crosswalks and busy corners with bikes and pedestrians. By stopping back from the stop line, all problems with conflict at intersections have reduced dramatically. Problems now equal zero.

The recent request to paint a chain of triangles behind the stop line has been a great help for motorists to observe our passive example of keeping a space cushion in those crosswalk areas where pedestrians don't stay between the lines. You can see these triangles at Francisco and Columbus by the Wharf and near UPS at 16th and Utah. Use of the horn has gone to zero, as have car horns directed at me. Operators with a reputation for dragging the line and who use the horn are, quite frankly, an embarrassment to me. If I am one of their passengers, I have had to leave their coach.

Diplomacy with coworkers is perhaps, at the end of the day, the biggest challenge to face with time behind the wheel. Did my hand signal to move up to the top of the zone at the terminal actually show a hostile flip-off with fingertips down in a condescending brush-off motion, or was it an alleluia, praise God, hands up, palms facing show of grace? I am reminded of how often it is not what is said, but the *tone* with which it is said.

# RUNNING TIME

Do my actions reflect my words? Do my words match my actions? Much of what I think about the quality of my job has to do with my perception of running time. I have had a core belief that the running time is not enough. Running time is the amount of time it takes to get from point A to point B. But if this is the case, then why have I been caught running ahead of schedule or arriving early? Perhaps I should say that the recovery time at the terminal is not enough.

Running time is how much time it takes to get from Ferry Plaza to Daly City on the 14 Mission; from Marina Green to Dogpatch on the 22 Fillmore; from SF General to CPMC Children's Hospital on the 33 Stanyan. Running time averages fifty minutes for most lines and runs. Recovery time is the miscellaneous time in minutes that is given at a terminal. The paddle may *say* we have ten minutes of recovery time at the end of the line, but if we are behind schedule by six minutes, we only have four minutes left to leave on time. I was reminded by an inspector in street ops that recovery time is what can put us back on time to leave on time so that headway is evenly spaced between coaches.

My resentment of schedules may not be shared by those who do not appear to be in conflict with running time. When I ask around about the rules for discipline and all I get back from my coworkers is, "I don't know because that has never come up," I stop in my tracks. When my boss tells me that other drivers never get any pass-up or running time violations, I have to ask myself why.

It is what I am doing right now as I type this into my computer. Why is trouble knocking at my door, and how can I keep this from repeating?

Accepting life on life's terms can give me a big laugh when I see how far off my thinking has strayed from reality. But if I have been granted time off by my boss, I need to look at this as an important message to reflect on why I am here and what I need to do to see my part in getting to this point. Paradoxically, the sweetest recovery time may come from unpaid days off!

The answer has to be my false belief about running time. I now see why inbound and outbound have been given those labels on crosstown routes that predominate at my bus barn. In the morning, inbound loads are heavy on the 22 going to Marina Green and light in the opposite direction. The same seems to hold true on the 24 line, which parallels the 22. And on the 49, the pattern remains the same, at least in the morning when inbound is heavy and outbound is lighter. This pattern also has me looking at my resentment for inbound running time. I get a break heading in the other direction. If I can wait for the next outbound terminal, I see that running time is restored.

I was told early on that I can't count on the terminal time as a given for a break time. My refusal to accept this may be the cause for most of my passenger complaints. I feel entitled to my ten minutes at the end of line, and if a passenger does not move to my liking, I have to watch my attitude.

I keep projecting my lack of time inbound onto my future trips, and I see that this is a form of hostage-taking that reduces my serenity. In the afternoon, I was having the same problem with my outbound trips. I couldn't see how I was expected to make all stops and maintain the schedule. Some days were light, and I would run ahead of schedule, and other days I was late and had no recovery time. My expectation about the running time had to be thrown out. There was no way all the delays could be built into the schedule in the peak direction, so my ability to predict my load was next to impossible. When passengers were giving me feedback about not having a problem with the bus line on a crosstown route, such as the 22, I realized my thoughts about running time needed a revision.

And so, as of this day, I will stop portraying myself as a victim of the schedule and see what happens. After all, when I hear my passengers playing the victim role about the schedule, I can see how they are being blind to their part in creating the problem. So, too, must I follow this example and not play a part in my own hell. Running time is what it is, and if it really is that bad, my coworkers will ask me about it. I just need to wait to see if my opinion is being solicited. The fact that the timetable does not match actual conditions is something to which I must adjust. I can only control what I can—my leaving time.

# LEAVING TIME

I was scolded for leaving North Point late on the 49 line by about four minutes. My leader went out of service in front of me at the biggest transfer point on Market Street. An angry mob piled out of her bus and onto mine. Her poles were still up, and I pulled into the zone right behind her. After words about how I handled the situation, I came to see that there were no 47s to be seen in front or back of me all along Van Ness Avenue. It was a hell of a Monday morning for the commute. But I made it work and reached the inbound terminal only four minutes down. I took the ten minutes the paddle allowed.

I knew that, no matter what I said or did in my passenger complaint review, I wasn't going to get off without some form of time-off or discipline. I have learned not to argue or blame others during times like this. I have also learned not to get defensive. Having seen this response in others, the effect it creates is one of guilt and denial. My approach is to give the "devil" what he wants and hope he moves on to greener pastures. The devil in this case being in the details of why I left late and how impossible it is to argue a point when no one listens.

It was not until several months later that I understood the dispatchers at the Kirkland Division were giving the 47 line a no-priority status in filling the runs. This makes for overcrowded 49 buses, and the common question asked at bus stops along the way is, "When is the next 47?" After receiving complaints from an angry public about overcrowding and reprimands from my boss about being late, I now perk up much faster when I hear the same question being asked by intending passengers on the curb. If I hear on Van Ness, "Where is the 47?" or "Can I take you to the train station?" I will be more proactive on the radio and in miscellaneous requests to make sure my boss knows about this. It means buses from another division are missing, and the chances for a complaint go up.

There is a fine line between calling attention to myself and just accepting a condition in headway. But if the condition persists for more than one week, I need to take action. The choice to fill out a miscellaneous or make a radio record sometimes baffles me as to whether or not it is an advantageous action or a waste of time. These choices make life as a transit operator interesting, to say the least. And, if there is one distinction we make as veteran operators of Zen within the railway, it is that distinction between *interesting* and *surprising*. Interesting makes for a good day. Surprises just won't do. Surprises are for birthday parties at home or under the tree on the December 24th. They are not welcome when it comes to making an appearance at the bus barn, even when they are supposed to be good surprises. For a bus driver, the best surprise is no surprise.

So it should come as no surprise that leaving late is not a good thing, particularly when an ADA complaint is involved. I now take the approach that any paperwork I create or any trail I leave is one that leads to no surprises. This starts as soon as I sit down in the seat at the beginning of my day.

Mirrors have a good view? Check. Doors open and close okay? Check. Rope tension firm? Check. Seat adjustable? Check. Air and brakes okay? Check. The best defense is a good offense. *This is run 379 calling for a radio check. Loud and clear.* Check.

# SPLITS

Of the three shifts an operator can choose to work, the day shift is usually a split shift. Senior runs during the day report at a time interval between 6:30 a.m. to 7:00 a.m. and get off twelve hours later. In the middle of the platform or drive time is a two-hour lunch. I try to plan these break times in such a way that the direction the bus is headed when I am relieved is favorable to where I choose to take lunch, meet friends, or run errands. Nothing is as simple as staying on the same bus I was just driving to shave off wait time or travel time to my lunch-time destination. If I have to go to another place to start my second part, I make sure the bus I am catching is also headed in the direction of where I make relief.

If I have to step off my bus to take another one in another direction, the extra cost in time adds up over the life of the sign-up. Also, the travel time to the second point can be half an hour away, so that combined together almost an hour of lunch could be consumed by riding other buses. I try to avoid this and pick break times that start and end close to places I frequent for lunch.

The Potrero Barn seems to be in the best location for finding the most diverse places to eat, shop, or meet friends for lunch. And from what my coworkers tell me, parking is not too bad. I try to get as much done on my lunch break as possible. The great thing about a schedule with a twelve-hour range is that you really don't ever have to buy or maintain any street clothes. I put my uniform on at 5:30 a.m. and take it off around 10:00 p.m. I don't have the time to change after work if I am en route to meet friends or going to a meeting.

So I am in my uniform all day, five days a week. The good news is that I have new uniform parts waiting for me in the receiver's office. After several years, we build up enough time to add to uniform pieces to make do with our long days and busy schedule. That way, we don't have to keep washing them constantly. Splits also make time to do laundry, if I can get the inbound feng shui right on the dot when making relief. Staying on the same coach after relief helps. Is the bus headed in the best direction from the barn or from my house? These little nuances in time and direction add up over the life of a sign-up.

# DRIVE CAMERA: HORSESHOES AND HAND GRENADES

Whenever an abrupt stop or impact of any type jolts the coach, the camera mounted on the windscreen activates. When my coach skidded on one of those metal plates on the street with loose gravel, off went my camera. I alerted Central Control and all was well. I wonder how often these cameras are monitored and if they have any influence on our record. A recent incident put me on the radar for a drive cam view, and now I must be extremely aware of the effect I am having on my riders, as I have been tagged to receive any and all PSRs relating to my actions on the bus. But all is well because close encounters do not count against an operator, only contact with another vehicle or object. Just as in horseshoes or with hand grenades, close doesn't count. Usually. You may get "points" for being close, but you usually don't win the battle.

The last time I came under scrutiny was when I was doing the run from hell. But in this case, I have a sweet run; yet, I am letting my equipment get the better of me. I have become a cry-baby without realizing it. Assigned a small coach on a 14 line day run, I am becoming resentful of crowding at the back door, which drags me down on the line. This circumstance cannonballs into a heavier load with seniors who need more time to climb the steps and find a seat. It is now that I need to fetch myself up sharply and pay attention to my interior mirror. I started too soon, and a woman almost fell to the floor because I could not see her in my interior mirror.

Also, seats for seniors become scarce in the crunch zone, and arguments arise over who is needier of a front seat. This argument never ends well, and I try to do everything I know how to prevent a shut-down and a call for help. To me, this is a failure of the system. Why should all the paying, working people on the bus have to suffer for some ridiculous argument that no one will remember as soon as we get past 16<sup>th</sup>?

If a camera activates, I call Central Control or put in a "miscellaneous" to mark the event. In the rain with wet brakes and on a hill, the odds increase for a camera activation. But in turning into a crosswalk, I do need to leave a much larger space cushion so as to not offend any intending pedestrian. It is not enough that my bus does not cross into the crosswalk when turning with a pedestrian off the curb. The call for scoring in horseshoes, by being the closest to the post and touching the post, is not a "score" when someone pounds on the door.

I have matured through my experience of cell phone complaints being just three digits away. I have settled disputes for years without a camera recording everything I say and do. I am not familiar with getting a call on the radio about something observed on my coach that I may not have seen. All of these things create an added dimension I must adapt quickly to or lose my Zen. Close doesn't count. The enemy of my enemy is my friend. This Arabic quotation has become enshrined as an almost reverent proverb. But the prince who said this was decapitated by angry mobs when he got home. Hence, this title—*Keeping Zen*.

# STRAIGHT THROUGH

I usually work a split. These runs are from 6:00 a.m. to 6:00 p.m., or from 7:00 a.m. to 7:00 p.m. Monday through Friday. The question remains, *How can I have a life (ha!) by working a twelve-hour range during the day and keep my sanity?* My answer has been to cram as much as I can into the two-hour break in the middle of the day. Just like school bus drivers, many city transit companies break up the day with split day shifts. You take people to school or work, take a break after the peak period, and then come back to take people home. As I live in the city, I try to make this work. I try to get something done over lunch, so when I get off at 7:00 p.m., I can feel like I accomplished things without having to do more after work. This is because I can be totally drained after a twelve-hour range of driving in the city. There used to be standby time built into these ranges, but this has evaporated from our run choices.

It is politically unpopular to pay drivers when they are not in the seat, but I would like to point out that the cost of not offering some of this standby time may be increasing payroll costs indirectly. Right now, higher cap numbers are filling these day run splits. Can this be sustained, or will it result in more breakdowns and sick days? The dispatchers with experience say no. *Give them an inch and they'll take a mile,* seems to be the philosophy when it comes to paying senior operators' standby report or standby detail.

But I would disagree mainly because I am a senior operator, and I have seen this standby pay go away. There used to be ninety hours a day built into this standby report (SR) or standby detail (SD) on our barn range sheets. This had an effect on a few senior operators during a sign-up posting. They saw the new range sheets and decided to retire. Reduction of standby pay can reduce the longevity of operators.

One way to avoid this is to do a straight through. This means coming in really early, say at 4:00 or 5:00 a.m., and getting off before school lets out. Or, it may mean to make relief during a school trip in the afternoon and work till midnight or later. This of course means picking up the bar crowd or those with no place to go who fall asleep and use your bus as a shelter.

In the morning, you pick up folks with a purpose in their life. At night, you get the denizens of the deep. After 10:00 p.m. inbound on Mission, I see no purposeful souls waiting inbound for the bus. The same is true for inbound on the 49 after Market. There really are no paying customers with any sense of good, orderly direction going to any perceivable destination with purpose, except to sponge off of others or to gaffle intending drug buyers.

Straight through runs have also undergone pay cuts. They have shorter recovery time at the terminal and get off sooner. My point is that the schedule cannot be met because the shaving of time and money becomes too extreme, and on-time performance falls below 60 percent. This seems to be the effect that causes gaps in service.

The harmony of a fifteen-minute recovery time, allowing buses to leave on schedule, would create more even distribution of buses on the line. The cost of shaving down run pay has its price in bunching and missing coaches and a lack of operators available to do the job. There should be a direct correlation between run pay, time off, and on-time service, but by keeping scheduling underfunded and understaffed, accountability is lost. Therefore, blame can be assigned in a nebulous way, directly or indirectly blaming the operator.

As I update this chapter, a massive set of training classes is underway to augment 160 new hires into the system. This will have a beneficial effect on creating even headway and less waiting. But I do question the burn-out rate and retention rate with less to look forward to because run choices improve with seniority. A great run becomes not so great if the operator who signed onto the run as your leader goes out on "classified industrial," and the dispatcher cannot fill that run.

Having schedule choices that allow for equal recovery time would help tremendously; it's just as important as base rate pay discussion in any contract. Our new contract was just voted on, and it looks like it will pass. But having to guess which run will be feast or famine still exists as we look at less recovery time on our paddles.

I currently keep my Zen by working a twilight shift straight through, enjoying weekends off. So far, so good. And thank you for riding!

# OWLS AND TWILIGHTS

Owls are runs which start around 5:00 p.m. and go to 6:00 a.m. the next morning. Some late twilights start around 4:00 p.m. and get off in the wee hours of the morning. When starting these late shifts, a relief is made during a busy time. The bus is full and the air is stale. The coach is fully warmed-up and ready to go. Usually a quick check of the mirrors is all it takes. The day starts out busy, but traffic thins as the shift goes on; this makes for less stress as the shift continues. Less traffic means less stress, and fewer people riding means less stress on the right leg and knee working the power pedal and service brake. Less riders mean fewer stops. I can go past more than two bus stops (skip stops) because no one rings and no one is waiting.

I have found these runs to be quite enjoyable and easy on the life outside of this job. I don't have to set an alarm, and I have regular business hours to make appointments and get things done. The problem is with social life, as the middle of the shift is during prime time for socializing and going out. I have known a few "owls" (operators who work nights), and going to breakfast is a nice time and place to catch up. I guess the best thing about working nights is staying out of trouble and not spending money!

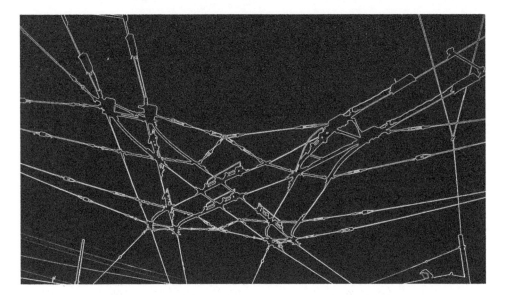

# THE TOWER

The second happiest moment of the day is usually the time we see the tower in our front windscreen because it means we made it back to the barn. We completed another day of revenue service without creating more "incident" paperwork or having trouble meet us before our day is done. Oh, just a minor piece of paperwork to be turned into the tower—the defect card. How long could this take? How bad could it be? Do you guys remember the recent movie title, *There Will Be Blood?*

The blood, sweat, and tears are very rarely are shed at the tower. These are found during special events when the bus is packed at 36 Avenue by Golden Gate Park, and there are another three miles of bus stops with people waiting to get on to go to BART at 5$^{th}$ Street. No, the tower is usually a sweet spot without drama.

The tears will come in the next week or the next month when you get the bus again on a cold, windy morning, and it still has no heat. Or the chair still loses air. You hop in and see perfectly through the eight mirrors, but halfway to Daly City, you become a low-rider in the seat and wish you had the hydraulics to lift your ass up to see what lies ahead. Or, the horn goes off each time you try to turn the wheel. (That poor little Chihuahua may never be the same again.) Glares and stares come from cyclists and pedestrians who think you are a regular horn honker. No, the art of the pull-in is to know what you can and cannot put on the defect card and what will or will not get fixed. This is much like reading tea leaves. But in this case, the leaves are the three parts of the defect card: yellow, pink, and white.

If you see lots of hanging chads by the door to the tower, you would do well to smile and let things go. After all, the logic within the hallowed walls of the tower may go something like, *If it was okay for you to drive like that all day, it couldn't be all that bad. If it was broken, you would have called for the road crew, and if it was unfixable, they would have sent you in.* Unspoken, to be sure and unwritten to be sure, but can you get your defect card on the windshield wiper with the order of "track 22?" Track 22 is code for that sinking feeling sometime during the next day when the next operator realizes they have been had because the manufacturer's maintenance schedule does not coincide with the parts budget allocation.

"Good one?" is the late-night request that comes forth from the tower when pulling in during the wee hours. A thumbs-up means to proceed to the happiest moment of the day, the fare box collector. Do not pass go. Do not collect 200 dollars. But on to free parking! (Actually no; parking is now paid, and it just went up.) Being able to get something fixed without breaking down on the road is truly a God-given gift. And to get the defect card on the wiper and to be assigned the same coach on the next day with no problems, is perhaps an eighth wonder of the world in keeping Zen as a transit operator in San Francisco.

# BEEP BEEP

Or, perhaps I should say, *Buwaaaahhh!* Each horn on each coach has a different sound. Each horn has a different sensitivity to pressure applied that's dependent upon how you tap or hit it. I usually tap the center of the steering wheel where the hub of the column is located. Usually, a single finger does not work. I have to pound it with a fist. But I also have to try different "parts of the clock" to see where the contact is made, just in case I need to know where to hit the hub to get a sound in a split second. An instructor would say that should never be the case.

Nor should I ever have to be in a traffic or pedestrian situation where a split second is required to sound the horn. We are trained to have a space cushion of eight seconds in the lane and to be at least four feet from parked vehicles. In scanning left-right-left every five to eight seconds, we should never theoretically be put into a compromising situation. So there should not be a knee-jerk, or, should I say, a thumb-jerk situation to sound the horn.

Nevertheless, covering the horn (as with the service brake) is always a good idea when crossing an intersection, crosswalk, or passing a streetcar or large delivery truck. There have been times when my thumb on the hub came in handy when someone attempted to walk between streetcars on Market without looking. I pray to my lucky stars when my intuition is working well, and I know when to expect trouble before it happens. Going for days on end without using the horn is a good sign I am following the rules of safe driving.

Sometimes, the horn goes off when I am not touching the horn button. This is extremely embarrassing for cars or pedestrians nearby. They think I am sounding the horn at them. I quickly move the steering column and adjust the wheel up and down. This stops the horn from blaring. I know I am making progress in solving coach defects when I can stay in service with a horn that stops going off randomly. Sometimes, I wonder about a ghost in or on the bus. If I try to fix a problem, and the problem goes away, then I relax. Sometimes, when a problem becomes intermittent, the timing seems uncanny, as if the bus were possessed with spirits. The horn is a good example of this. If I talk to the bus, the problem stops. If the problem comes back, I stop again.

I use the rule of threes. If I can't get the problem to go away for the third time, I call for the shop. I ask myself if I have been using the horn for the wrong reason. When in the Zen, the horn works fine. This relationship between my attitude and the working of the parts of the bus is a coincidence that I cannot ignore, especially with the shop.

When an operator goes out of service for a defective horn, they are following the rules. This qualifies as safety significant. I need to remember that I have been in that situation myself. I tested the horn after relief and found it did not sound off. I very rarely use it, so I continued my day. Upon pull-in at the tower, I sarcastically asked the shop man how to use the horn. He was new and did not take me seriously.

I pleaded with him to show me how to use the horn. I wanted to teach him a lesson. An experienced shop friend from within the tower came to the cab quietly. He slowly rocked the steering column up into the vertical position, using the joystick lever on the left. He then, ever so eloquently and majestically, lowered his pointer finger down on the center dial and sounded the horn, Oh, I was humiliated. Never get fresh with the shop. They can make you look really stupid. But that's when they smile, and I realize their experience goes a long way toward helping me understand how to correctly operate the equipment. I laughed so hard, I told them I was putting this in the book!

I can keep the Zen when I choose to see their problem as my own and that we are all one. Still, I can't help but feel like Wile E. Coyote when my "road runner" leader holds the horn down at a double-parked vehicle.

# SACRAMENTO

David Chui and John Campos are termed out as Supervisors (Alderman, City Council Member) within the city and are looking to move to Sacramento to become a part of the State Legislature. This is being written in February of 2014, Valentine's Day. Tom Ammiano, Mark Leno, and our previous mayor, Gavin Newsom, have also moved from city office to work for the state in Sacramento.

Nowhere does the lack of continuity between city and state seem so apparent than to operators behind the wheels of city transit. Muni is described by many in government and in the editorial columns of weekly rags as a "rogue" agency. Federal office holders also display public disdain toward our agency, such as during the Third Street Light Rail Project and its grand opening. A switch malfunctioned, and the angry crowd jeered at our then Director of Transportation, who was present for the ceremony.

More recently, a new hybrid bus broke down with our mayor on the coach for the inaugural of this new equipment. Notice a pattern? Lack of regular parts replacement and starvation of federal monies going to the agency from the State have dire consequences. Borrowing, begging, and paying Peter to pay Paul has put the MTA at an on-time performance level of 50 percent. Combining Operations with Maintenance could be the major cause of this.

In a recent *Examiner* article, this "half time" performance was no longer printed for a shock effect; it carried with it the *business as usual* attitude of matter-of-fact. But it is during these off-scheduled trips on the bus that the battle cry can go up by those waiting on the corner, and the odds of getting a complaint go way up. Most of my complaints stem from this fact alone: I have double or triple headway, and frustration builds up so much that an attempt to keep the bus from breaking down results in an angry pass-up complaint.

Federal rules allow for a depreciation schedule of twelve years for bus replacement. Our trolleys at Potrero are over twenty years old. The first set of hybrids was purchased at the trolley twelve year mark and the expiry for federal funds came and went with no purchase of sixty foot articulated trolleys, save for a piddling quantity of thirty-five placed in service in the mid-2000s. This is a shortfall of fifteen articulated trolleys from the previous order in 1991-93 of fifty that are now two decades old and counting. Wow, can we get a State Historic Vehicle license plate?

Is the density of San Francisco decreasing? Are there fewer tall residential buildings around town? Even though Supervisor Chris Daly managed to get monies from some of the developers of new tall buildings downtown before he left office, most of the residents-to-be may not be transit riders, but car people. A garage for their car does seem logical for anyone paying the small fortune it takes to buy a place here in the city. To fork over a million and still have no place for a car, does seem a bit extreme. But extreme is what we are talking about here.

One person in the planning department completely believed his lie that the downtown tunnel had not the capacity for five car trains. Our Boeing-Vertol railcars could be hooked together five car lengths in the Market Street tunnel. Our Breda streetcars can only be hooked in twos or as a single car. This lowered commute capacity has resulted in extra motor coaches on the N-Judah and 5 Fulton lines or a 7 Rapid on weekends, but only after years of running packed cars.

And so to keep this *Transit First* and *City That Knows How* philosophy alive and not play a cry-baby, I will focus on a few transit corridors that need state help. Our precious life blood of elected officers who are leaving the city for Sacramento must please be aware of how they can help. We had such a great resource in Willie L. Brown, Esq., who had been a leader of the state legislative body, and then our mayor. Construction of a much-needed crosstown downtown tunnel was made into reality from fantasy. Stuff got done.

"Da Mayor" was awarded by naming the new East Bay span of the Bay Bridge after himself. He almost forgot to bring the sign to the ceremony. I have a plausible reason. He didn't want to be associated with a twenty-five-year, billion dollar project that still kept the problem intact. The bolts holding it together were cracked and vulnerable.

I guess the good news is that the central subway will need another name. I think Willie should have waited for the tunnel to be named after him. Perhaps the project is no longer popular with the public, but it should be. Ask anyone from Union Street who has to take the 45 through Chinatown. This tunnel would be a fantastic crunch zone saver, but only if it is extended past Broadway.

Though people complain and cry as they are wont to do, whether it be about a fantastic Art Museum from the Fischer family on the quad in the Presidio or a stately campus off the Golden Gate Bridge approach from our *Star Wars* hero, George Lucas, so, too, do people cry about the crosstown tunnel or a high-speed rail line to Anaheim. But there will always be cry-babies. True leadership makes stuff happen because of a vision of the future that takes inevitabilities into account toward their conclusions. And the conclusions are more shocking than those of the whiners. Our population and transit system needs cannot be ignored. Investment should to be made now because it won't get any cheaper in the future.

And so it goes—this missive entitled "Sacramento." New sewer lines and Bus Rapid Transit median lanes on Van Ness are 3 years away at best. We don't need history to repeat itself with cracked frames on our new trolleys from driving over rough pavement. The right lane, lane 3, from Broadway to Lombard may need a new concrete base because so much time has passed since the last repaving.

Although I desire a tunnel system under these federal and state highways, this is where a BRT or Bus Rapid Transit Lane is needed. But in the current configuration, a loss of a lane on these roads could add to delays. The median has been worked on at least three times since the last repaving. The median should be removed, along with the parked cars, so we can have *real transit lanes* on this federal highway.

We have seen much-needed HOV lanes installed on US 101 North to Santa Rosa, but no such diamond lanes have been added to the highways within the city. The Golden Gate Bridge has a lower deck preinstalled for transit, but the new parkway approach was built with absolutely no public discussion about a transit lane for Golden Gate Transit or for a rail line from Fisherman's Wharf or from 19th Avenue.

In short, we don't need a BRT for Geary Boulevard; ask the riders—the 38 is okay. We need a BRT along 101 on Van Ness and for 19th Avenue (State Highway 1), perhaps one for Lombard (US 101), one for the approach to Crissy Field, and one for the Golden Gate. The biggest need for BRT is actually on the weekends. If we wish to attract people from the Central Valley in the summertime (when they want to beat the heat) to our city, we could use smooth movement on our clogged arteries. Our city is water-locked on three sides by bridges, and as such, a toll for driving into the city on a weekend could be monitored and paid for by a fast track system installed in a driver's smart phone application. Technology is the key. Getting others to see how sweet this variable rate penalty can be to speed flow and traffic remains out of touch for now.

I am not a politician, so I don't understand the call for free parking on Sundays, but if you look at the projected numbers of population growth and the building in progress, it does seem to change the poverty-consciousness or budget restraint for transit. The ulterior motive of this book is to try to raise consciousness about the *transit first* label applied to San Francisco and to look at life from the point of view of a transit operator. Oh, and by the way, "Thank you for riding!"

# LINE TRAINER

After training in the classroom, the cadet trainee gets to finish up by driving in revenue service with an operator observing him/her behind the wheel. This can be done by the observer sitting in the first curbside seat from the door. If the coach fills up, and no seats are left for seniors, I have learned it is still best to vacate the first seat and stand in the aisle, holding on to the rails near the front door for support. As an observer, I can then become a curbside ambassador by stepping onto the sidewalk and making sure seniors get the support they need and look to the rear for any late runners. This turns a potentially negative situation over lack of seat space into a pleasant line training experience.

Most new operators need help in answering questions for directions. The timing of being asked a question can be disruptive to an operator's concentration. As a trainer, I sometimes wait and see if the student can answer the question. If in a safe zone, I pose a question that commonly gets asked. I let students know when and where questions usually get asked, so they can learn to answer as quickly as possible without being distracted. This is important when crossing through special work in the overhead. This advice, my division instructor says, is the number-one assist a line trainer can give to a new hire.

There are two new training division instructors in the office this week. They are beaming at me, as both were operators working at a barn I was at when they were driving. The previous division instructor reminded me that I would be needed as a line trainer when the next class was to be augmented into the division. Maybe the hunt for a new patch is not the answer, except for being of service to another, regardless of the rules or their infractions. Driving on the Mission line has caused many a bus driver to change career midlife because the trouble in the aisles becomes too much to bear on a regular basis. Indifference and apathy creep into our psyches.

The other line training operators still may need help with their coach. I must remember why I am here—to be of service and to help out whenever or wherever necessary. Humility is perhaps one of the best spiritual tools for keeping Zen as a trainer and as a transit operator.

# LOST AND FOUND

It takes a certain earnestness to make a commitment to read a book of essays by a bus driver, with this exposition being no exception. What am I saying? The journey to publish a book has shown me who the avid readers are, the state of the brick and mortar bookstore, and the online mega monster that is as large as a subtropical river delta in South America— Amazon! It has also brought me back to the door-to-door sales mentality when I was a young Scout.

Carrying around my newly-published book for sale is not unlike the cold call of door knocking and selling movie tickets as a Boy Scout raising money for new tents for our troop. The interplay of selling self to another in a compressed time frame is truly a Gemini trait that ranges through almost every emotion and sense of self-esteem and self-worth.

The number-one question on people's minds when they find out I am a Muni bus driver is *What is the craziest thing that happened to you on the bus?* And I tell them about the spread-eagle Folsom fair-goer, in nothing but chaps, who jumped onto the front of the bus, holding onto the windshield wipers and bike rack, and baring his all to the riders and those at the stop. Or, there was the time in the Inner Mission when I was offered a loaded crack pipe placed on the fare box, with a lighter as fare payment. Hmm … do tell.

I understand the mission statement of Balboa Press, which is to be a nature-friendly, new age publisher. Does a publisher in Bloomington, Indiana desire to publish everything that goes on inside a Muni bus, especially on the back seat? The addition of cameras on all buses has been a mixed bag. And so goes the range of emotion in promoting myself and editing for interest and genre category. I guess this is a good time to state, "The views contained herein do not necessarily reflect those of the SFMTA or its employees."

The first book, *Finding Zen,* has a preface I wrote. This sequel, *Keeping Zen,* has an epilogue containing an update on attitudes about our transit future. I also wanted a chapter in book one that had an air of finality to it, such as, "When Worlds Collide." The idea came to me at Sacramento and Fillmore on the 22 line. Lost and found!

I had lost this idea in my head because I didn't write it down when it came to me. Fortunately, I got the idea back upon awakening. I had *found* the idea again. Indeed, the items found on a bus were as diverse as the riders, and the thoughts and emotions about such seemed worthy as a chapter with an intriguing conversation angle. If you want to start an interesting conversation with bus drivers, ask them about their most interesting lost and found story.

So back to the Fillmore on the 22.

I had returned a Mac Book Pro to a woman who had left it on the bus. This was at Jackson, an affluent neighborhood where the bus is relatively empty. She had been on the cell phone and was distracted by the attention given to the caller. She forgot the fact that she had her computer with her. A passenger alerted me to the laptop left on a seat at the back of the bus by the rear door. I immediately called on the radio, stating my run, line, and coach number. Operations Central Control would be able to locate my bus, should the rider call 3-1-1 about leaving an item onboard. I never describe the item in full on the air, so that only the owner would be able to identify it when Central calls me back. But the call-back never came. I put the computer in my bag out of sight for safe keeping. Placing a laptop on the dash certainly would not do.

When I pulled in, I talked to the dispatcher about what to do. The laptop's owner's phone numbers were on a business card inside the sleeve of the computer's cover. We called the number but got no answer. When we have an item for lost and found, we are to tag the item with our cap number, coach number, and line in which we found the item. We leave the item to be picked up the next day by the mail room to have it sent to the main lost and found department at S. Van Ness and Market.

The dispatcher was hesitant to leave the computer on the console by the other lost and found items overnight, and said I could return the item to her, as I lived close by. This was a rare event in my employment in that I was being trusted to do the right thing. I returned the laptop to her that next evening at the front door of my building. Returning an item to you, its owner, is fun. I love the look on your face when you are reunited with your cell phone, computer, or billfold.

But not so for the dispatcher once the superintendent found out what had happened. Many times, a call for thanks for an above and beyond action carries discipline, not commendation. By describing my action in returning the laptop off-property as a commendation, the dispatcher was scolded by our boss for not following protocol. The dispatcher may have received some time off for this. I never saw him at the desk again. I must follow the wisdom that the rules contain for my own protection and the protection of the railway.

Most of my actions of knighthood and chivalry seem not to be welcome in this age of Tina Turner's verse captured in *Beyond Thunderdome*. The lyric rings true for a bus driver in San Francisco, "We don't need another hero!" Even so, I relish the challenge a found item can have.

Here's another example. A loaded wallet is in the gutter in front of me as I pull up on Mission at Third. A back-and-forth homeless rider on the sidewalk spots the wallet in the gutter seconds after I do. But I am closer to it, and I pop the brake and snatch the wallet just seconds before she gets to it. And it is here that I am confronted with my own prejudice and fear revolving around lost and found.

Who am I to say if the homeless woman on the street is more or less a help in returning the wallet to the owner than I am? Her desire for a reward for doing the right thing is as valuable or assured as my wish, if that be the case. Why am I so predisposed to assume she would follow the law of the sea better or worse than I would? The law being, *finders, keepers, losers, weepers.* Many would feel entitled to keep the cash as a sort of finder's fee and expect gratitude for returning the license and credit cards.

In this instance, her license showed an address very close to the line and easy to ride by on my way home. I stayed off the air about it and gave the wallet to the doorman in her building after I pulled in. She had already alerted Muni about the wallet, but didn't know when she had lost it.

The curb by the back door is another common collection point for lost belongings, but technically, doesn't qualify as railway property. This gets into the issue of what constitutes a bus stop and the zone considered to be our responsibility as a driver. Anything within four feet of the bus zone is part of our responsibility, such as with intending passengers and the determination of pass-up.

This gets to the core of why I love this job. I am confronted about my own beliefs and values by the diverse sedimentation of deposits laying all around me and at a bus stop. Is the dispatcher's fear of leaving the laptop in the office any different than the fear I have that a wallet and the cash inside will disappear before or after the mail room employee comes to pick it up? Can the trust of Lost and Found or another employee be higher or lower than the trust of a person on the street? The opening of the heart reveals so much more.

One sweet grandma had left the entire contents of her wallet with coin purse on the bus, containing about six paper dollars and heavy change. I described the item to Central as soon as I found it on the seat where she had been sitting across from me. She was waiting for me on the other side when I came back outbound.

"I am sorry I can't give you anything for returning this," she said in a gentle voice. "Oh, but you have," I responded without hesitation. The feeling of reward without monetary consideration is such a wonderful feeling. True abundance may be found without counting money. Once I start pondering on the dollar amount of where *finders, keepers* becomes the reward theory, I am already in trouble. Trouble with karma, trouble with dharma. I also question my belief as to why a wallet loaded with twenties is *less valuable* as a return item than a coin purse full of nickels and pennies. The thought that some young tech professional does not need her twenties, as much as a senior needs her pennies, is a value judgment based on assumptions that may not have any basis in reality.

And it gets back to the difference between the second and third grade. Second graders want what they want, and they want it now! Third graders realize that listening and believing the first thought that pops into their heads may not be good or have a good outcome. Everyone needs to be taught that the first thought that comes into our mind should not necessarily be acted upon. This becomes no more evident than in the dialogue of a crack addict or meth-head on the bus mumbling or shouting in the seat behind me. When impulse becomes primary, the circuit breaker of thinking about our thinking gets lost or turned off. This results in bad decision-making! God bless the angels who come our way on the bus.

The number one, big-ticket tech items lost are cell phones. Smart phones are left behind when the passenger falls asleep. Most of us are so connected to our smart phone that the likelihood of leaving it behind has recently become rare. Stolen is more like it. Older cells are easily returnable because they are unlocked.

I can wait for a call to come in, pop the brake, step off the coach, and give the bus number and location of my coach, so a friend can meet and intercept. Usually, the owner is with the friend, as they are asking the friend to call their phone to see if someone answers. I love returning this item because it frees me up from making a lost and found tag when I pull in. as the item has never left railway property, I can't get in trouble for not following protocol.

Other times, a savvy rider realizes the item was on the bus, and they wait in the other direction to scan for me and the item on the seat. Either they find the item where they left it, or I hold the item in my hand as I approach the stop. The look of relief on their face is worth at least two or three profane disruptions that may also occur that day. It is interesting, though, to note that the quality of the day is based on the energy I am putting out, and that good deeds and disruptions have a difficult time happening close together or side by side, if you will. By keeping the Zen, I may be keeping the problems at bay. In this case, somewhere near Pier 90.

# DUST COVER JACKET

"Do you have a car?" you may ask. Yes, I do, and you're sitting in it! Today's car number is 5481. I get a new car every day, and I can hold up to sixty people at once. I get to take you where you want to go and get paid to do it. I don't have to worry about parking, and I can call on my radio for help from crews of people set up to keep me going. I don't have to pay for gas because this car uses free power from the O'Shaunessy Dam at the Hetch Hetchy Reservoir. Parking is free, and I have a camera to send a bill to someone blocking my parking space. If there is any trouble, I can call for help from my phone, and it can be here in three minutes. The police are my friends; coworkers are also here to help.

I sold my truck when I moved to San Francisco to pay for the deposit on my apartment, and I haven't had to pay for tires, batteries, gas, parking, or insurance since I got rid of it. My employer is my insurance company. The money is coming in—not going out. I enjoy driving very much and am glad that I am not polluting the air while I'm driving you to where you need to go. It's kind of like the ultimate in ride share without any carbon emission. Thanks for riding in my car today!

# GLOSSARY

**defect card:** a card carried with transfers and run timetable, that an operator can mark off during pre-op inspection, after pull-out, or on the road in revenue service and can take the coach out-of-service if deemed unfit by the shop on a road call initiated by operations, or a street inspector who can ask the driver to pull the coach in or wait for a coach trade from another operator, contacted by radio, so as to minimize wait time in headway between buses.

**kneeler:** pneumatic pistons installed at the front door of a coach that can lower the steps for those needing assistance in placing a load or themselves onto the first step.

**lift:** a device located below the front steps of a bus that extends out from the bus an onto the sidewalk to allow for a rolled object, such as a wheel chair, grocery cart, or stroller, to be loaded up to the aisle elevation without using the steps.

**avenues:** numbered streets located out by Ocean Beach in the Sunset and Richmond neighborhoods of San Francisco.

**streets:** numbered roads close in to the city in the Financial District, the Mission, and area south of Market, or SOMA.

**islands:** a set of land tips in the most remote location of the world, in the center of the Pacific Ocean, where a stressed-out bus driver sometimes goes in his mind, renamed since established in the Western world by the Earl of Sandwich. Or, those concrete medians on Market Street with a bus stop that takes you south of Golden Gate Park to the Inner and Outer Sunset or to an inbound terminal short of the Ferry Plaza.

**curbs:** referring to the stops on Market Street, downtown, which take you north of Golden Gate Park and can get you west much faster than the islands on a weekend when there's a special event.

**crunch zone:** a time and place to avoid in the aisle, as items may get picked, or a fight or altercation may arise. The chances of a bus breakdown are high.

**over there:** a phrase to be avoided when addressing an operator. An answer of yes or no still results in no clarity about where to stand or wait for another bus.

**flat tire:** a blemish or flattened tread in a city transit bus tire that can create a thumping noise at speeds over 15 mph.

**hot lunch:** excreted body fluids on a seat or floor on a bus.

**running time:** the amount of time allowed to be spent on a treadmill at the gym on lunch break. Or, the amount of time it takes to complete a trip on a run.

**leaving time:** used by Operations and Central Control to mark a time for a revenue or shop appointment for an in-service coach, usually by the inbound terminal. Commonly refers to time on paddle that denotes time for a coach to start a trip inbound or outbound.

**splits:** day shift that allows for a two-hour break in the middle of the shift.

**feng shui:** literal translation: wind-water: that ancient practice of harmonizing with invisible energies.

**straight through:** a shift with no break, save for some recovery time written-in on the paddle, which may or may not be true in reality.

**owl:** run that works from 9:00 p.m. to 6:00 a.m.

**open run:** no operator scheduled in front of you. (See ninth level of hell or packed, stacked, and racked, in first book, *Finding Zen*.)

**timed transfer:** a vanishing point, but still followed on the 22 Fillmore at Mission at night. The 22s will wait and see if a 14 is coming so you can make the transfer. The 38 and 90 seldom make this, as with the L and 90. Get that run number!

**lojong:** the mind training practice in Tibetan Buddhist tradition that treats disaster or adversity as a way to overcome trouble and pain by using the Fifty-nine Slogans.

**the wiggle:** a well-marked bike route connecting the Panhandle with Market Street, thereby avoiding any hills.

**e p u:** auxiliary or battery mode whereby a trolley is not connected to the wires.

**l p o:** late pull-out.

**a p c:** automatic passenger counter; can be spotted by the red laser lights on either side of the steps or above the door by the courtesy lights.

**v t t:** verified transit training, in which a professional Class B operator within a city transit system is re-qualified on a bi-annual basis, it's a distinction from tour bus endorsement that carries no v t t card.

**range sheets:** posted in the Gilley or break room at the barn where the line and run and bus pull out.

**g s u:** general sign-up, whereby an operator can change report barn; it may mean use of different equipment or mode.

**safety significant:** any coach defect that would contribute to danger to life and limb.

# SONG OF THE TROLLEY MAN

**Douglas Meriwether**

I've seen them all:
Young and bold
Appear like a spark,
Then depart as I start
To read the latest tag
In the back rag
By the half-drunk can
Wrapped in a bag.
The ancient ones,
Full of mold and scold
Or just plain old,
Short and fat,
Or pleasantly plump.
Mind the start, mind
The bump.
As I walk the dog and creep away
From the curb; *do not disturb,*
Says the pass around the neck.
"Wait till I sit!"
(Prevent a fit.)
That says, *I made it*
*Up the steps!*
"Step up, please!"
"Yes sir, yes ma'am!"
I've seen them all:
Short and fat,
Thin and tall,
Soft, rosy cheeks,

Eyes of merriment,
Eyes of distress,
Eyes of joy,
Eyes that are coy.
Yokes and cuts,
Blokes and mutts,
Bosoms and bubble butts,
Grannies, *Mujercitas*
On the Mission.
Grasping sometimes,
Clutching the rail.
With the smile of a mile,
The old Filipino men
Of Mac Arthurs's song:
*I will return, I'll be back,*
Their ball caps proud.
Or wait for the next bus,
If too large a crowd.
A Gemini refrain:
Girls, these buses are like men
In life;
Don't worry,
There's always another one coming along!
"Hey, that 'music is too loud!
Turn it down!"
With a trolley man's frown—
Stare, actually,
The moonie, stone face
Reaching that far-off place
We go to ... we go
To return to sane,
To alleviate the pain
Of a thousand greasy wheels,
Of a thousand scratchy windows,
Of a thousand aimless fluids
Transmuted by a thousand asses

Sitting on a thousand dirty seats.
I sing the song of the Trolley Man.
Oh, you got your
Sunflower seeds
On the floor
By the door.
Cigarette butts,
Bubble gums wrapped,
A transfer in a thousand dirty pieces,
A day pass, Golden Arches remnants,
Taco Bell, dipping dot hell,
Coffee cups, coffee lids, coffee stirrers,
Needle bent, Condom spent,
Tiny zip-lock bags once containing
A fifteen-year relapse.
To keep the tweak (or)
The wake up (for),
To keep the freak
At Bay
(Or) The Marina
(Or) The Trans bay
(Or) The Ferry Plaza
(Or) Wherever, whenever the hell
They go.
Like cockroaches when the lights come on.
I see all, give a ride
To all.
I am the Trolley Man.
The walk of shame in the morning after,
The dark, bug-eye glasses,
The hide of the passes,
Or
The hall of fame after winning another game,
A high-five as victors!
I am the vicar, the mayor, the
Bus Driver,

Who picks you up
Or wakes you up,
At the end of the line.
Engine, engine 49
Going down the Van Ness line.
If the trolley goes off the track,
Do you want your money back?
"Last stop people!"
I go no further
Than the truth
Of your ability to read
My head sign,
My sun sign,
By design.
Shall I put up *Garage*?
Isn't it great
To put in a request?
I've ordered a grande refill
Sitting at my table
At Starbucks.
The current ambiance:
Off-day convenience.
Ah, the buzz
Of the only pleasure left.
No punctuation worries,
No schoolmarm duress
Of creative process.
And so I sing the song
Of the trolley woman
Of the trolley man
From the barn,
Where expert operators
Remain.
Potrero,
Which is Spanish
For little field

Or meadow—
A patch of brown grass
Near a freeway by-pass,
A hillock, actually,
Near Union 76 gas,
Firm on Serpentine
Like a Chinese fire drill—
The New Year's Dragon.
Do we gracefully
Glide
Down the old Mission trail.
Hidalgo's brave stand
From Hermosillo and Sonora
All the way to Yerba Buena
Towards the Mission of San Rafael.
Delores, do we glide
Our sixty foot trolleys
Side-by-side
With lo-riders,
Subarus,
And asshole SUVs
With TCP stencils.
Tráfico,
Tráfico,
The Ebb and Flow:
Keeping our pride
And our asses
Away from the curb.
Not to lose the wires,
Not to drop our poles,
And so it goes.
The operators
Of Potrero in
Turns and twists
Born from new lists
To exist,

Not resist.
To be regrooved,
Retread, reworn,
Reshod anew—
To Sit Back
And Watch the Show!

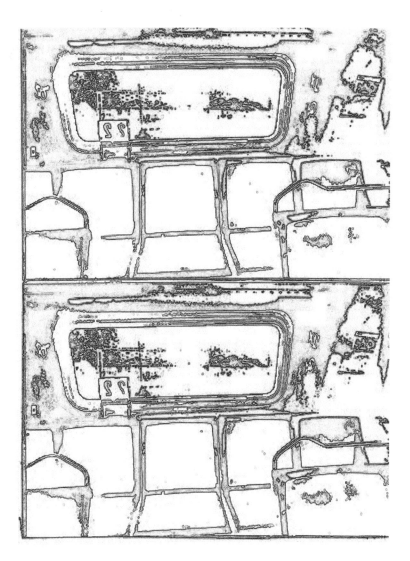